ISRAEL and the
NATIONS in PROPHECY

By the same author . . .

THE LIVING GOD

ISRAEL and the NATIONS in PROPHECY

by Richard W. DeHaan
Teacher of the Radio Bible Class

Foreword by Dr. Lehman Strauss

ZONDERVAN PUBLISHING HOUSE

GRAND RAPIDS, MICHIGAN

ISRAEL AND THE NATIONS IN PROPHECY

Printed in the United States of America

FOREWORD

Reading the galley sheets of Richard DeHaan's latest book, ISRAEL AND THE NATIONS IN PROPHECY, was a delightful and refreshing experience. Following so closely the Arab-Israeli war of 1967 one might expect to find at least a little of the spectacular or sensational. But such is not the case. On the contrary, these eleven chapters comprise a sound and sane presentation of numerous prophetic Scriptures.

Commencing with God's unconditional promises to Abraham, continuing with the striking prophecies of Daniel and Ezekiel, and concluding with the final overthrow of Russia at the Second Coming of our Lord Jesus Christ, the writer traces the course of history as God has revealed it within the confines of His holy Word.

Richard DeHaan is not prophesying; he is teaching the prophetic Scriptures, and in this volume he has done a fine job of it. In Chapter One alone I noted the use of more than forty verses of Scripture from both the Old and New Testaments in which the teacher expounds his subject.

Is Israel's claim to Palestine a legitimate one? Are the Gentile world powers identified? Does the Common Market in Europe have prophetic significance? Is there a sound basis for the claims of British-Israelism? Is there a future repentance and restoration for Israel? These and many more questions of interest are answered in this timely book.

The Radio Bible Class is fortunate in having as its teacher one who is following in the tradition of its famed founder, Dr. M. R. DeHaan.

LEHMAN STRAUSS
1968

PREFACE

With Israel and other nations of the Middle East occupying a strategic role in the world situation today, there is a natural interest in whether or not the present picture has prophetic significance. All, however, do not see eye-to-eye in interpreting the events that are taking place. Some would tell us that the Jews are not Israelites, and various theories concerning the true identification of the "ten lost tribes" are being advanced, with impressive-looking genealogical records offered as proof. Others, conceding that present-day Jews do indeed bear a historical connection with the twelve tribes of Israel, contend that their status as a nation and their presence in Palestine have no real prophetic significance. They say that God is through with Israel as a nation, and that we must recognize today only a spiritual seed of Abraham as the people of God.

This book seriously examines the Scriptures to determine the identity of the "seed of Abraham," and then sets forth in clear and understandable terms a general picture of that which will transpire in the end-time. Throughout the entire study the redemptive aspect of God's program is emphasized. The supernatural defeat of Russia and the hate-inspired cruelty of Antichrist are set forth in their prophetic perspective.

The believer who reads these studies will see evidence that the great events predicted by the prophets may soon be fulfilled, but he will also be guarded against date-setting or a fanatical "other-worldliness." He will be stimulated to live every day in readiness for the return of the Lord Jesus, and will be strengthened as he realizes anew that God and His people will be victorious in the end.

It is my prayer that these prophetic messages will enlighten and encourage God's people in these latter days.

Grateful acknowledgment is given to Mr. Herbert Vander Lugt, Radio Bible Class Research Editor, to Mr. A. Clair Hess, Radio Bible Class Publications Editor, and to Miss Helen Baxter who typed the manuscripts. Without their valued contributions the publication of this book would not have been possible.

I am thankful for the opportunity of sending forth this volume, and trust that it might bring honor to "God, even the Father of our Lord Jesus Christ, the Father of mercies, and the God of all comfort, who comforteth us in all our tribulation" (II Corinthians 1:3, 4).

RICHARD DeHAAN

CONTENTS

Foreword . . . . Lehman Strauss

Preface

1. The Seed of Abraham 13

2. The Times of the Gentiles 27

3. The Western League of Nations 39

4. British-Israelism Examined 51

5. The Land of Canaan 75

6. Israel's Seventy Weeks 83

7. Israel's Repentance and Restorations 93

8. Three Decisive Wars 105

9. Russia's Crushing Defeat 117

10. The Time of Russia's Overthrow 127

11. The Manner of Russia's Overthrow 137

ISRAEL and the
NATIONS in PROPHECY

Chapter One

THE SEED OF ABRAHAM

The Jewish people of the world are the subject of much discussion these days. We read articles in a variety of periodicals that speak eloquently of their genius, their loyalty, their sterling character, their fairness even to those who hate them, and their sacrificial devotion to certain ideals. On the other hand, our country is flooded with virulent literature picturing them as a fiendish people who are behind a great deal of violence and crime, who control the world's wealth, and who instigate the anti-Christian programs in Communistic nations. Some even contend that Hitler's persecution was directed by Jews who desired to purge from their own midst certain of their enemies.

As is often the case, the truth lies between these two extremes. Not everything the Jews have done can be justified. Nor have they as a people revealed a tolerant (much less sympathetic) attitude toward the Gospel. However, those who publicize their "hate material" against the Jews are guilty of distorting the facts to build a case against these people. We who are Christians need not overlook the wrongs done by the Jews, but we certainly must deplore the fact that they are so bitterly maligned. As we think of their history since A.D. 70, when Titus and his Roman armies destroyed Jerusalem and the Temple, we are ashamed

13

of the way some "Christians" have persecuted them. However, we also recognize that this is precisely what God through Moses declared would happen to them because of their unbelief. Moses, the man perhaps revered by the Jews more than any other, prophesied both their spiritual apostasy and the suffering it would bring upon them. Five chapters of Deuteronomy are devoted to the pronouncements of blessings for obedience and curses for disobedience. Moses demanded a definite decision for or against God, although by revelation he knew the people would forsake God and be chastened by Him. In Deuteronomy 31:29 we read,

> For I know that after my death ye will utterly corrupt yourselves, and turn aside from the way which I have commanded you, and evil will befall you in the latter days; because ye will do evil in the sight of the Lord, to provoke him to anger through the work of your hands.

Many divinely anointed prophets followed Moses in Jewish history. These Old Testament preachers made predictions to their wicked contemporaries of impending judgments from God, and the records of history confirm the accuracy of their pronouncements. They foretold with amazing exactness the birth, the life, the death, and the resurrection of Jesus Christ. They also made solemn declarations concerning events that have not yet been fulfilled, but which will occur in connection with the second advent of our Savior. The Old Testament prophetic Scriptures give us a detailed picture of confederacies of specific nations, and of the role they will fill in God's end-time program. It is fascinating to observe the international scene, and to see things moving toward the final fulfillment of these great prophetic pronouncements.

Who Are the People of Promise?

Though Gentile nations will play an important role in the end-time and will be recipients of great blessing during the millennial age, the center of God's prophetic program is Israel. All who accept a literal interpretation of the prophetic Scriptures will agree with this. The problem we face is that of identifying Israel. The vast majority of our present-day scholars do not question that the Jews are the physical descendants of the twelve tribes. Some small splinter groups can be found who deny this, although among them there is little agreement concerning the identity of present-day Israelites. Some point to the Anglo-Saxons, others to the Negroes, and still others to the American Indians.

National Future for the Jews?

Some serious Bible students who recognize the Jews today as the physical descendants of the Israelites deny that they have a divinely predicted national future. They declare that because the Jews rejected Jesus Christ they have forfeited the blessings predicted by the prophets, and that the Church is now the true Israel of God. Among them are those who believe that the people of Israel will experience a great national turning to God shortly before the return of Jesus Christ, but they do not believe that the promises of national blessing in the land of Canaan will be fulfilled. They look for a spiritual renewal among the Israelites, but believe that Jesus took the kingdom away from Israel because the leaders and people rejected Him.

We, however, are convinced that the Jews are the physical descendants of Israel, that they will as a nation turn to Christ, and also that they will occupy the central place in the millennial age when Jesus Christ personally brings to this earth universal peace, prosperity, and justice.

In this chapter we will examine the promise to Abraham to see just what it contains, and then we will carefully consider what the Bible means when it speaks of the "seed of Abraham."

THE ABRAHAMIC COVENANT

The covenant God made with Abraham is looked upon by all Bible scholars as of paramount importance in any study of Bible prophecy. It marks a significant change in God's program. Up until this time He had revealed Himself to all mankind, but men had demonstrated their depravity by ignoring Him and going their own wicked way. The first eleven chapters of Genesis clearly reveal this fact. God therefore chose now to reveal Himself in a special way to one man, and from this one man to certain of His descendants who would become a unique nation, and from this nation to the peoples of the world. It was never God's intention to be the God of only one nation. This will be borne out clearly as we proceed in our study.

God's covenant with Abraham was first made as recorded in Genesis 12:1-3. It was repeated to him and amplified somewhat on three later occasions: Genesis 13:14-17; 15:1-7; and 17:1-18. Still later God reiterated the same promises to Isaac and Jacob.

The first enunciation of the Abrahamic covenant is to be found in Genesis 12:1-3,

> Now the Lord had said unto Abram, Get thee out of thy country, and from thy kindred, and from thy father's house, unto a land that I will show thee;
> And I will make of thee a great nation, and I will bless thee, and make thy name great; and thou shalt be a blessing.

And I will bless them that bless thee, and curse him that curseth thee: and in thee shall all families of the earth be blessed.

PROMISES TO ABRAHAM

God assured Abraham that He would do four things for him. He declared that: (1) He would produce from Abraham a great nation, (2) He would bless him, (3) He would make his name great, and (4) He would make him a blessing to all the families of the earth.

These promises were all literally fulfilled. The nation of Israel descended from Abraham, great wealth and prosperity attended his life, his name was and is honored among many of earth's peoples, including Jews, Mohammedans, and Christians; and through Christ all the families of the earth have been blessed.

Moreover, when God repeated the covenant to Abraham with some amplifications, He also promised him that he would be "a father of many nations" (Genesis 17:4), declaring,

And I will make thee exceedingly fruitful, and I will make nations of thee, and kings shall come out of thee (Genesis 17:6).

These promises too were literally fulfilled. Through Ishmael, through the sons of Keturah (Genesis 25:1, 2), and through Esau, he became the father of kings and many nations.

PROMISES TO ABRAHAM'S SEED

God also made specific promises to Abraham's seed. While God promised Abraham that nations and kings would come from Him, it is obvious that the greatest blessings centered about one special nation, which would be great

(Genesis 12:3), and beyond numbering (Genesis 13:16; 15:5). God declared that He would grant the land of Canaan as an everlasting possession to this specific nation. Therefore, although the descendants of Abraham, other than those in the line of Isaac and Jacob, are honored as part of Abraham's family, the promise of Canaan is limited to one particular line. God plainly told Abraham that "in Isaac shall thy seed be called" (Genesis 21:12). Later God clearly indicated to Rebekah, Isaac's wife, that the special promise would be carried on through the younger of the twin boys that had not yet been born.

> And the Lord said unto her, Two nations are in thy womb, and two manner of people shall be born of thee; and the one people shall be stronger than the other people; and the elder shall serve the younger (Genesis 25:23).

Jacob, not Esau, was destined to be the father of that special nation to whom a unique relationship to God and an everlasting possession of the land of Canaan is promised. Jacob's sons became the progenitors of the twelve tribes of Israel. They have a place in God's program that is distinctive, and they possess promises that do not apply to the other descendants of Abraham.

Having noted that there is this distinction between the posterity of Abraham in the Old Testament, we are now prepared to consider some of the New Testament statements concerning the seed of Abraham.

New Testament Teaching

The Apostle Paul reaffirms the contrast between the seed of promise and those who are merely physical descendants of Abraham in Romans 9:7 where he quotes from Genesis 21:12.

Neither, because they are the seed of Abraham, are they all children, but, In Isaac shall thy seed be called.

The Lord Jesus emphatically declared to the Jewish leaders that even those who were descendants of Abraham through Isaac and Jacob did not possess the fullness of blessing without true faith. In other words, mere physical descent through the chosen line was not enough. To enjoy the full blessings of the Abrahamic covenant one had to be a genuine believer. The proud Pharisees of Christ's day boasted about their lineage from Abraham. Jesus acknowledged their proper physical relationship when He said, "I know that ye are Abraham's seed . . ." (John 8:37). However, He then went on to deny their spiritual relationship to Abraham by saying,

. . . If ye were Abraham's children, ye would do the works of Abraham (John 8:39).

Paul expressed the same truth when he said, "For they are not all Israel, that are of Israel." This means that though Israel as a nation has certain glorious promises regarding the land of Canaan and a special relationship to God, only those individuals who truly believe in Him will enjoy the full blessings of the Abrahamic covenant. Those who possess genuine faith are saved and will inherit the promised blessings. This is the spiritual element, the true remnant, within the chosen line.

Gentile believers are also the seed of Abraham. Paul states this in Galatians 3:6-9,

Even as Abraham believed God, and it was accounted to him for righteousness.

Know ye, therefore, that they who are of faith, the same are the sons of Abraham.

And the scripture, foreseeing that God would justify the

Gentiles through faith, preached before the gospel unto Abraham, saying, In thee shall all nations be blessed.

So, then, they who are of faith are blessed with faithful Abraham.

The Gentiles who receive Jesus Christ are "heirs according to promise" (Galatians 3:29). This does not mean that such believers will inherit the promise of the land of Canaan, but that they who are Abraham's spiritual seed have entered into that aspect of the promise which applied to "all the families of the earth."

The seed of Abraham is fourfold:

1. There are his physical descendants through Keturah, Ishmael, and Esau who became the ancestors of kings and nations, and to whom the promise of the land of Canaan does not apply.

2. There is the line of promise through Isaac, Jacob and his twelve sons from whom the nation of Israel came.

3. There is the spiritual seed within this chosen line, those who truly believed in God, obeyed His Law, and experienced salvation even in Old Testament days. Among those who have died, only those who were saved by faith will share in the blessedness of the new Jerusalem, and only those living Israelites who are saved at the time the Lord Jesus comes to establish His kingdom will enter into the earthly millennium.

4. There are the spiritual descendants of Abraham who are not Israelites, but who have entered into the blessing of the promise, ". . . and in thee shall all the families of the earth be blessed."

Therefore, though we recognize that Gentile believers are among the "seed of Abraham," we by no means see this as in any sense an indication that the promises to Israel have been canceled. Only those who fail to recognize the Biblical distinctives within the seed of Abraham will make this error. It is imperative, therefore, that every Bible student recognize that the "seed of Abraham" does not always have reference to the same group of people.

GOD'S PROMISES LITERALLY FULFILLED

We have already called attention to the fact that God's promises to Abraham were actually realized. He achieved great wealth, universal fame, and became the father of many nations. God's declaration, "I will bless them that bless thee, and curse him that curseth thee" (Genesis 12:3) has been fulfilled literally, both in the life of Abraham and the nation of Israel. History testifies to the fact that those nations which showed kindness to Israel have been blessed, while those that persecuted the Jews have suffered disastrous results. There is only one promise in the entire Abrahamic covenant that has not been literally fulfilled beyond question. This one exception is found in the words of Genesis 17:8,

> And I will give unto thee, and to thy seed after thee, the land wherein thou art a sojourner, all the land of Canaan, for an everlasting possession; and I will be their God.

The fact that every other promise was realized in an absolutely literal manner, should give pause to any Bible student who begins to spiritualize these words by making Canaan a symbol of Heaven. God was speaking to Abraham about an earthly territory which his physical descendants would possess. There is no question about the identity of the "seed of Abraham" to whom this promise was made. The land of Canaan was not given to Ishmael, to the sons of Keturah, or to Esau. They were assigned other territories. It is not the possession of the purely spiritual seed of Abraham; that is, Gentile believers who have entered into the blessing of "all the families of the earth." The land of Canaan was given specifically to the line from Abraham through Isaac and Jacob.

> . . . for in Isaac shall thy seed be called (Genesis 21:12).
>
> And not only this, but when Rebecca also had conceived by one, even by our father, Isaac
> (For the children being not yet born, neither having done any good or evil, that the purpose of God according to election might stand, not of works, but of him that calleth),
> It was said unto her, The elder shall serve the younger.
> As it is written, Jacob have I loved, but Esau have I hated (Romans 9:10-13).

PROMISES TO ISRAEL STILL IN FORCE

That Gentile believers are the spiritual seed of Abraham in no way changes this promise to Israel. The Bible not only distinguishes between the fourfold seed of Abraham, but also carefully denotes to which division the specific promises apply. The descendants of Ishmael, Keturah, and Esau are not to claim the promises made to Israel. They received their own special blessings. The unbelieving Israelite will not receive the same inheritance as the one who lives a life of obedience and faith. Nor can Gentile believers who are the spiritual seed of Abraham lay claim to the promise of the land of Canaan. As God's Heavenly people, we have a distinctive place in His program. The promise of Canaan belongs to Israel, and to Israel alone.

CANAAN, AN EVERLASTING POSSESSION

One problem remains to be answered in this discussion of the seed of Abraham. It is the promise of the land of

Canaan to Israel as an "everlasting possession." Many Bible students have pointed out that the land of Canaan will not exist forever as it stands today. They correctly observe that according to the New Testament Scriptures the present earth-system will be burned, and that it will be replaced by the new heavens and new earth. Peter declares,

> But the day of the Lord will come as a thief in the night, in which the heavens shall pass away with a great noise, and the elements shall melt with fervent heat; the earth also, and the works that are in it, shall be burned up.
> . . . we, according to his promise, look for new heavens and a new earth, in which dwelleth righteousness (II Peter 3:10, 13).

Moreover, the new earth will be the eternal resting place for the New Jerusalem, which is 1500 miles in length and breadth and height (Revelation 21). This will require a vastly enlarged and different globe from our planet as it exists today. Then, too, the new earth will have no sea (Revelation 21:1). Therefore, even though the Jews will occupy and control all of Palestine during the 1000-year earthly reign of Jesus Christ, they will not have it forever. How then can one speak of the land of Canaan as an everlasting possession?

Millennium Connects Time and Eternity

The answer to this question is found in recognizing the fact that the Bible views the mediatorial millennial kingdom of Christ as the door into the universal eternal kingdom of God. The present earth-system will be burned, and the new heavens and earth will come in its place as described in Revelation 20 and 21.

> And I saw a great white throne, and him that sat on it, from whose face the earth and the heaven fled away, and there was found no place for them.
>
> And I saw a new heaven and a new earth; for the first heaven and the first earth were passed away, and there was no more sea (Revelation 20:11; 21:1).

On this new earth God will fulfill His promise to Israel that she will have a distinct national identity and territory forever.

THE THRONE OF DAVID

Thus it will be also with the "throne of David" which the angel promised to Mary's virgin-born Son.

> . . . and the Lord God shall give unto him the throne of his father David.
>
> And he shall reign over the house of Jacob forever; and of his kingdom there shall be no end (Luke 1:32, 33).

The earthly throne of David will not be abolished, but will merge into the eternal throne in the new earth. There is good reason to believe that David will, under the supervising mediatorial kingship of Jesus Christ, rule over Israel during the millennium (Isaiah 55:3, 4; Jeremiah 30:9; 33:15, 17, 20, 21; Ezekiel 34:23, 24; 37:24, 25; Hosea 3:5; Amos 9:11). On the new earth Israel will still be distinct, and have her own king — perhaps David.

The Lord Jesus Christ will leave His throne as the mediatorial King to take His place on the *one* eternal throne, "the throne of God and the Lamb" (Revelation 22:3), thus bringing the mediatorial Kingdom to an end as it leads into the eternal kingdom of God in the new heaven and the new earth. He will continue to exercise His regal authority, but will do so as the eternal Son with the Father in the unity of the Godhead. It is because the prophets saw the earthly kingdom as a prelude to the eternal kingdom of God that they spoke of it as eternal, and sometimes, as in Isaiah 65: 17, they viewed the new heavens and new earth in close connection with the millennial kingdom on this present earth.

As long as this earth stands in its present form, Israel holds the divine title-deed to the entire land of Canaan. In that sense it is *forever*. This use of the word "forever" is illustrated by the slave who requested that his ear be bored as a token of his desire to continue as the servant of a beloved master, and thereby indicated that he would "serve him forever" (Exodus 21:6). He did not mean that the master-slave relationship would be continued on the other side of death. *Forever* in this case meant as long as both of them lived. Thus, the land of Canaan belongs to the Jews through all time as an earthly possession, and in eternity will still be theirs on the new earth, though transfigured and much enlarged.

Chapter Two

THE TIMES OF THE GENTILES

In the Arab-Israeli war of 1967 the Jews regained possession of old Jerusalem, the section which Jordan had held up to that time, and took control of the site where the temple once stood. Many Christians wondered how this sudden development related to the prophecy our Lord made in Luke 21.

> . . . and Jerusalem shall be trodden down by the Gentiles, until the times of the Gentiles be fulfilled (Luke 21:24).

Did it mean that "the times of the Gentiles" had come to a close? Were we to assume, because Jerusalem was no longer under Gentile dominion, that the return of Jesus Christ must occur within a very brief period of time? To answer these questions intelligently we must first of all define exactly what the Bible means by the term, "the times of the Gentiles," and we must carefully consider the words of Jesus in their setting.

As we approach this subject, it is well to bear in mind that the word "Gentile" in both the Old and New Testaments designated the non-Jewish peoples of the world. The "times of the Gentiles" is then a period during which God carries out a program with those who are not Israelites.

God, who has outlined a specific plan for Israel, has revealed a program for the Gentile nations as well.

NEBUCHADNEZZAR'S DREAM

The expression, "times of the Gentiles," is found in Luke 21:24, and the Bible elsewhere makes abundantly clear when it began and when it shall end. The book of Daniel gives us the picture of four great Gentile world powers which must rise and fall before Christ establishes His universal earthly kingdom. In Daniel 2:31-36 we read the prophet's description of Nebuchadnezzar's dream.

> Thou, O king, sawest, and behold a great image. This great image, whose brightness was excellent, stood before thee, and the form of it was terrible.
> This image's head was of fine gold, its breast and its arms of silver, its belly and its thighs of bronze,
> Its legs of iron, its feet part of iron and part of clay.
> Thou sawest until a stone was cut out without hands, which smote the image upon its feet that were of iron and clay, and broke them to pieces.
> Then were the iron, the clay, the bronze, the silver, and the gold, broken to pieces together, and became like the chaff of the summer threshing floors; and the wind carried them away, that no place was found for them; and the stone that smote the image became a great mountain, and filled the whole earth.
> This is the dream, and we will tell its interpretation before the king.

God gave to this heathen ruler Nebuchadnezzar a view of these four great world empires from the human standpoint. He saw a great image of a man, colossal and magnificent. It was *one* image, a picture of world unity centered around man, not God. Daniel interpreted Nebuchadnezzar's dream as follows:

Thou, O king, art a king of kings; for the God of heaven hath given thee a kingdom, power, and strength, and glory.

And wherever the children of men dwell, the beasts of the field and the fowls of the heavens hath he given into thine hand, and hath made thee ruler over them all. Thou art this head of gold.

And after thee shall rise another kingdom inferior to thee, and another third kingdom of bronze, which shall bear rule over all the earth.

And the fourth kingdom shall be strong as iron, forasmuch as iron breaketh in pieces and subdueth all things; and, as iron that breaketh all these, shall it break in pieces and bruise (Daniel 2:37-40).

DANIEL'S VISION

In Daniel 7 we have another view of these same kingdoms, but this time from God's standpoint rather than man's.

In the first year of Belshazzar, king of Babylon, Daniel had a dream and visions of his head upon his bed; then he wrote the dream, and told the sum of the matters.

Daniel spoke and said, I saw in my vision by night, and, behold, the four winds of the heaven strove unto the great sea.

And four great beasts came up from the sea, diverse one from another.

The first was like a lion, and had eagle's wings; I beheld till its wings were plucked, and it was lifted up from the earth, and made stand upon the feet as a man; and a man's heart was given to it.

And, behold, another beast, a second, like a bear, and it raised up itself on one side, and it had three ribs in the mouth of it between its teeth; and they said thus unto it, Arise, devour much flesh.

After this I beheld, and, lo, another, like a leopard, which had upon its back four wings of a fowl; the beast had also four heads, and dominion was given to it.

After this I saw in the night visions, and, behold, a fourth beast, dreadful and terrible, and strong exceedingly, and it had great iron teeth; it devoured and broke in pieces, and stamped the residue with its feet; and it was diverse from all the beasts that were before it, and it had ten horns.

I considered the horns, and, behold, there came among

them another little horn, before which there were three of
the first horns plucked up by the roots; and, behold, in this
horn were eyes like the eyes of man, and a mouth speaking
great things (Daniel 7:1-8).

In Daniel's vision, these kingdoms are revealed as bestial,
sub-human and brutal. All their outward glory does not
hide their real nature from God.

END OF GENTILE DOMINION

Both in Nebuchadnezzar's dream and in Daniel's vision
the destruction of these kingdoms is portrayed. Nebuchadnezzar saw a stone crash against the image, smiting it to
bits, and then the stone suddenly became a great mountain
that filled the entire earth. Daniel said,

> Thou sawest until a stone was cut out without hands, which
> smote the image upon its feet that were of iron and clay, and
> broke them to pieces.
> Then were the iron, the clay, the bronze, the silver, and
> the gold, broken to pieces together, and became like the chaff
> of the summer threshing floors; and the wind carried them
> away, that no place was found for them; and the stone that
> smote the image became a great mountain, and filled the
> whole earth (Daniel 2:34, 35).

CHRIST TAKES COMMAND

Daniel saw far more than the stone smiting and destroying the image. He saw the Ancient of Days taking over
the kingdoms of the world. He saw man, true man represented in the Son of Man, assuming the reins of human
government, for he declares in Daniel 7,

> I saw in the night visions, and, behold, one like the Son of
> man came with the clouds of heaven, and came to the Ancient
> of days, and they brought him near before him.
> And there was given him dominion, and glory, and a

kingdom, that all people, nations, and languages should serve him; his dominion is an everlasting dominion, which shall not pass away, and his kingdom that which shall not be destroyed (Daniel 7:13, 14).

GENTILE POWERS IDENTIFIED

It is not difficult to identify the four world powers depicted in the dream and vision. Daniel expressly declared to Nebuchadnezzar, "Thou art this head of gold" (Daniel 2:38). Daniel 5 closes with the words, "And Darius, the Mede, took the kingdom, being about three-score and two years old." In the eighth chapter both Medo-Persia and Greece are named as kingdoms that will succeed Babylon. The fourth kingdom is not specifically named, but since the historical records so clearly declare that Babylon, Medo-Persia, Greece, and Rome succeeded one another as world powers, there is no question as to the identity of the legs of iron and the terrible beast. It has reference to the Roman Empire.

THE FUTURE ASPECT

This last phase of Nebuchadnezzar's dream and Daniel's vision has posed a problem for many Bible students. In the dream the stone destroyed the Roman Empire with a sudden and cataclysmic blow, and immediately filled the earth with its presence. In the vision the Ancient of Days took over the reins of human government. This seems contrary to historical fact. The Roman Empire never was suddenly destroyed. It continued for several hundred years after the Lord Jesus came to earth, died, and ascended into Heaven. A combination of factors — immorality, weakening home life, and spiritual darkness — gradually led to the decay of this mighty empire until barbarian armies finally brought about its fall. (In a later study we will explain the significance of the destroying stone, identify the Ancient of Days, and indicate when this part of the prophecy will be fulfilled.)

The final destruction of Gentile world power as described by Daniel is therefore still future, and it is obvious that a long period of time separates the fourth kingdom in its first phase from the final 10-part form. The vision itself gives no indication of this long time-lapse. The best explanation of this is found in a recognition that God did not give Daniel or the other Old Testament prophets an understanding of the Church Age, the age of grace which spans the time from Christ's first advent to His return. The Old Testament Scriptures predicted our Lord's birth, death, resurrection, ascension, present position at God's right hand, and His glorious return, but gave no indication of the length of time involved between His ascension and return in glory. If we understand this, many questions concerning Bible prophecy are answered. When we recognize that Bible prophecy passes over this interim period without filling in details, we can see why the Scriptures present no specific prediction concerning the United States of America and many other prominent nations in the world today. Prophecy deals with those events connected with our Lord's first coming, and with those that will occur during the brief period just before He returns in glory. Some modern nations, like Russia, are mentioned in the prophetic Scriptures, but only as they relate to Israel in the period immediately preceding the return of Jesus Christ to rule over the earth. It is for this reason that we must be very careful in the interpretation of prophecy. The Lord has not revealed any details that will enable men to set an approximate date for the rapture of the Church.

FIRST AND LAST PHASES OF GENTILE DOMINION

The times of the Gentiles began when Nebuchadnezzar captured Jerusalem about 600 B.C. Ever since that time Jerusalem has been under Gentile dominion, until 1967 when the Israeli were successful in recapturing it. We do not know how long the Jews will be able to maintain control of it. It is possible that pressure will be put upon Israel to abandon this part of the city. Moreover, the rapture of the Church is also imminent, and therefore could take place at any moment. When this happens, the Jews will return to the land of Palestine in great numbers, and enjoy freedom for three and one-half years. However, Daniel 9:27 tells us that the political world ruler will suddenly enter into Jerusalem, take over the temple, and initiate the most horrible period of persecution against the Jews that the world has ever seen. (A more complete treatment of this is to be found in Chapter Six.)

THE PRESENT SITUATION

On the basis of these observations we must not read too much significance into the fact that the Jews at the present time are occupying the ancient city of Jerusalem. Prophecy does not deal specifically with the Church Age. A careful reading of Luke 21:20-24 reveals that our Lord foretold the destruction of Jerusalem, which was accomplished by Titus and the Roman armies in 70 A.D., and then declared that Jerusalem would be under Gentile dominion "until the times of the Gentiles be fulfilled."

> And when ye shall see Jerusalem compassed with armies, then know that its desolation is near.
> Then let them who are in Judaea flee to the mountains; and let them who are in the midst of it depart; and let not them that are in the countries enter into it.

> For these are the days of vengeance, that all things which are written may be fulfilled.
>
> But woe unto them that are with child, and to them that nurse children, in those days! For there shall be great distress in the land, and wrath upon this people.
>
> And they shall fall by the edge of the sword, and shall be led away captive into all nations; and Jerusalem shall be trodden down by the Gentiles, until the times of the Gentiles be fulfilled (Luke 21:20-24).

The words immediately following describe the signs which will be manifested just before Jesus Christ returns to reign over the earth (Luke 21:25-28). The Lord gave no explanation of the time period that would elapse between the destruction of Jerusalem and His glorious return. The Lord Jesus was aware of Old Testament prophecies which declared that the Jews would return to Palestine, and in the state of unbelief rebuild their temple in Jerusalem. He certainly knew that they would dwell for a time, while in unbelief, feeling secure as prophesied in Ezekiel 38:8. However, He also knew that this would only be temporary, and that when He would return to reign over the earth Jerusalem would be under the domination of Gentile oppressors.

The Apostle Paul also recognized that the Jews would rebuild their temple, and that the political world ruler of the end-time would seize it and demand that men worship him there.

> Let no man deceive you by any means; for that day shall not come, except there come the falling away first, and that man of sin be revealed, the son of perdition,
>
> Who opposeth and exalteth himself above all that is called God, or that is worshiped, so that he, as God, sitteth in the temple of God, showing himself that he is God (II Thessalonians 2:3, 4).

It is therefore necessary to recognize that the Jews will have temporary possession of the city before Antichrist turns against them.

In other words, the occupation of Jerusalem by the Jews as we see it today is not a contradiction of our Lord's prophecy, nor does it necessarily indicate that the return of Jesus Christ must occur within a few months. Our Lord simply declared that the Jews will not have *permanent* control of this city until "the times of the Gentiles" has been ended. It is certain that the Jews will not retain direction over the city of Jerusalem indefinitely. During the last half of the tribulation period it will be under Gentile dominion. God's ancient people cannot permanently possess this sacred city until they turn to Christ and submit to His rule.

The "times of the Gentiles" began about 600 B.C. and will end when Jesus Christ comes in glory to rule over the earth from Jerusalem.

> Behold, the days come, saith the Lord, that I will raise unto David a righteous Branch, and a King shall reign and prosper, and shall execute justice and righteousness in the earth.
>
> In his days Judah shall be saved, and Israel shall dwell safely; and this is his name whereby he shall be called, THE LORD OUR RIGHTEOUSNESS (Jeremiah 23:5, 6).

Although there are no prophecies concerning specific nations during this intervening Church Age, some characteristics of "the times of the Gentiles" are set forth.

DECLINING GLORY

Nebuchadnezzar's dream indicated that the four successive empires would become increasingly strong but gradually deteriorate in splendor. Gold is heavier and more precious than silver, silver than brass, and brass than iron. History attests to the fact that each of the succeeding governments was stronger than the preceding one, though less glorious. Rome, the fourth world power, was by far the strongest, best organized, and most efficient of these empires, but it lacked the glory and luster of Babylon, Medo-Persia, and Greece. This decline in quality has marked the entire era of Gentile dominion.

UNGODLINESS

When Nebuchadnezzar demanded that everyone worship the golden image he had made or die (Daniel 3) he set a pattern that has marked the entire age of Gentile dominion. He rejected the one true God, and world leaders ever since for the most part have either ignored or rebelled against the one true God. Even in today's turbulent times, very few of the world's leaders acknowledge God, the God who has revealed Himself in the Bible.

IDOLIZATION OF MAN

Another mark of Gentile world dominion is the worship or deification of man. In Nebuchadnezzar's demand for self-worship we recognize a precedent that has repeated itself ever since that time. In some cultures like Japan and China we have seen the worship of emperors and ancestors. The final ungodly world ruler will demand that men worship him, for Revelation 13:8 declares,

> And all that dwell upon the earth shall worship him, whose names are not written in the book of life of the Lamb slain from the foundation of the world.

Moreover, modern man, though looking upon himself as originating in the slime of a primordial past, exalts himself to the place where he is his own god. He insists he doesn't need God, and lives in disobedience to His laws. Man does not want the one true God.

HOSTILITY TOWARD ISRAEL

"The times of the Gentiles" is also characterized by hatred and persecution of Israel. This was foreshadowed in the attempt to destroy Daniel's three friends, and the casting of Daniel into the den of lions. The history of Gentile world dominion is marked by an intense hatred of the Jews and repeated efforts to exterminate them. When one remembers how Titus and his Roman armies slaughtered them, and how Hitler with his henchmen ruthlessly killed almost six million of them, he cannot help but marvel at their indestructibility. In between these two events literally hundreds and thousands of Jews have been slaughtered or expelled from the lands in which they lived. As "the times of the Gentiles" draws to its close the Jews will again experience a most terrible time of persecution, the worst in their history. According to Zechariah 13:8 an intensive campaign of extermination will effect the destruction of two-thirds of the Jews then living in the land of Palestine. In fact, when the nations gather to fight the last battle before Christ comes, their purpose will be to utterly destroy the Jews who have turned to God during the Great Tribulation. It is at this precise time that Jesus Christ will come to defeat the rebellious nations and establish His righteous rule over the earth.

> For I will gather all nations against Jerusalem to battle; and the city shall be taken, and the houses rifled, and the women ravished; and half of the city shall go forth into captivity, and the residue of the people shall not be cut off from the city.

> Then shall the Lord go forth, and fight against those nations, as when he fought in the day of battle.
>
> And his feet shall stand in that day upon the mount of Olives. . . .
>
> And the Lord shall be king over all the earth; in that day shall there be one Lord, and his name one (Zechariah 14:2-4, 9).

When this prophecy is fulfilled, the "times of the Gentiles" will have run its course and come to an end. Christ's establishment as King will inaugurate God's program of millennial blessing.

Chapter Three

THE WESTERN LEAGUE OF NATIONS

The prophetic Scriptures speak of a day when the nations will be under a world ruler who will achieve political (Revelation 13:7), commercial (Revelation 13:17), and religious (Revelation 13:15) world unity for a very brief period of time. It is not our purpose here to enter into a detailed discussion of the dictator, but to determine what the Bible declares about his empire. Many have speculated concerning the place the United States may have in this future confederation of nations under the Antichrist. Others have wondered why it is sometimes spoken of as the revived Roman Empire, and have wondered if this means that the boundaries of this alignment of nations will correspond exactly to that of the ancient Roman Empire at the time it reached its zenith.

As we study this subject we will consider those Scripture passages which specifically foretell a coming league of ten nations. We will discover that nothing has taken place in the past that can be properly considered a fulfillment of these prophecies. It will also become apparent as we go along that this coming power bears a relationship to the Roman Empire of the past.

Nebuchadnezzar's Dream

Daniel 2 records the description of Nebuchadnezzar's

dream as it was revealed to Daniel, along with his explanation of its significance. Nebuchadnezzar saw a huge image which had a head of gold, breast and arms of silver, abdominal region of brass, and legs of iron, with its feet a mixture of iron and clay. In our last chapter we had no difficulty concluding that the image portrayed the four successive Gentile world empires — Babylon, Medo-Persia, Greece, and Rome. There is general agreement among Bible scholars upon this matter.

THE SMITING STONE

It is in the understanding of the concluding scene of Nebuchadnezzar's dream that we encounter a variety of interpretive ideas. Nebuchadnezzar's dream closed with the appearance of a stone rolling down from a mountain, striking the image at its feet, pulverizing it, and then growing suddenly into a huge mountain which filled the entire earth. Here are Daniel's words concerning the king's dream,

> Thou, O king, sawest, and behold a great image. This great image, whose brightness was excellent, stood before thee, and the form of it was terrible.
>
> This image's head was of fine gold, its breast and its arms of silver, its belly and its thighs of bronze,
>
> Its legs of iron, its feet part of iron and part of clay.
>
> Thou sawest until a stone was cut out without hands, which smote the image upon its feet that were of iron and clay, and broke them to pieces.
>
> Then were the iron, the clay, the bronze, the silver, and the gold, broken to pieces together, and became like the chaff of the summer threshing floors; and the wind carried them away, that no place was found for them; and the stone that smote the image became a great mountain, and filled the whole earth (Daniel 2:31-35).

Many Bible students have suggested that the stone represents Jesus Christ in His first coming. They declare that He by His life, death, and resurrection defeated Satan and provided for the ultimate conquest of all the forces arrayed against God's people. This interpretation is rather difficult to accept because it is too general, and moves from a description of literal earthly kingdoms to a completely non-literal and spiritual sphere. For the most part these interpreters believe the Church is the means by which God overcomes these hostile powers until they are completely subjugated by Jesus Christ at His return. Again, it is well to point out that the Church had no significant part in the destruction of the Roman Empire, and that Rome deteriorated slowly for several centuries before barbarian armies invaded it and brought about its fall. This dream, however, does not present the downfall of the Roman Empire in such a gradual manner. The image was destroyed suddenly and overwhelmingly. Therefore, unless one is ready to despair of finding a literal and precise fulfillment of this prophecy, he cannot accept the above interpretation.

FUTURE FULFILLMENT

We who believe Bible prophecy will be literally fulfilled know that nothing in history can be truly looked upon as the realization of the "stone aspect" of this dream. Therefore, we expect the final "feet stage" of this image to appear sometime in the future, and we believe it will then suffer a sudden cataclysmic destruction just as we have it described in Daniel 2:34, 35. Inasmuch as two feet would normally have ten toes we see a ten-nation confederacy *implied*.

DANIEL'S VISION

The second passage of Scripture bearing upon this future league of ten nations is Daniel 7. Daniel records a vision

God gave him depicting the same empires that Nebuchadnezzar's dream foretold. The dream of the king presented these empires from a *human* standpoint, but Daniel's vision depicted them in their true character as God sees them, cruel and rapacious. The lion, bear, leopard, and the "beast, dreadful and terrible" represent the Babylonian, Medo-Persian, Grecian, and Roman Empires respectively. Again, it is in connection with the fourth empire that some details of the vision present problems to Bible students. Here is Daniel's account pertaining to the fourth empire,

> After this I saw in the night visions, and, behold, a fourth beast, dreadful and terrible, and strong exceedingly, and it had great iron teeth; it devoured and broke in pieces, and stamped the residue with its feet; and it was diverse from all the beasts that were before it, and it had ten horns.
> I considered the horns, and, behold, there came up among them another little horn, before which there were three of the first horns plucked up by the roots; and, behold, in this horn were eyes like the eyes of man, and a mouth speaking great things (Daniel 7:7, 8).

WHAT ABOUT THESE HORNS?

Even as we naturally wonder what the ten horns represent, and would like to know who or what is signified by the "little horn" which uproots the three others, and then "speaks great things," so did Daniel (Daniel 7:15-22). Therefore, God gave him some further information:

> Thus he said, The fourth beast shall be the fourth kingdom upon earth, which shall be diverse from all kingdoms, and shall devour the whole earth, and shall tread it down, and break it in pieces.
> And the ten horns out of this kingdom are ten kings that shall arise; and another shall rise after them, and he shall be diverse from the first, and he shall subdue three kings.

And he shall speak great words against the most High, and shall wear out the saints of the most High, and think to change the times and the laws; and they shall be given into his hand until a time and times and the dividing of time.

But the judgment shall sit; and they shall take away his dominion, to consume and to destroy it unto the end.

And the kingdom and dominion, and the greatness of the kingdom under the whole heaven, shall be given to the people of the saints of the most High, whose kingdom is an everlasting kingdom, and all dominions shall serve and obey him (Daniel 7:23-27).

God's Answer

God informed Daniel that the ten horns on the fourth beast represented the ten kings (political leaders and their realms) that will rise to power. The "little horn" signifies a political ruler who will come to the front, subduing three heads of state in the process, and apparently securing the submission of the other seven. He will be arrogant, presumptuous, blasphemous, and a bitter enemy of God and His people. He will rule for "a time and times and the dividing of time" (three and one-half years), and then he will be personally judged and his kingdom destroyed by the "Ancient of days" (Daniel 7:9-14, 26-27).

Ten Kingdoms

Here again we have ten kingdoms presented just as they are implied in the feet of Nebuchadnezzar's image. They appear on the world scene simultaneously, and co-exist with the "little horn," though they are subject to him. Since this is true, all efforts to make these ten horns represent ten successive kings in ancient history are obviously in error. These ten horns do not come up one by one, each standing alone, but are in their place together. Nothing that has ever occurred in history corresponds to this picture. Furthermore, the destruction of this blasphemous "little horn" is by the "Ancient of Days," and ushers in a universal and everlasting kingdom. Therefore, any person who takes prophecy seriously must recognize that this ten-horn stage of the fourth beast is still future, and that the rise of these kingdoms and the arrogant "little horn" will occur just before Jesus Christ returns to establish His kingdom.

John's Vision of the Beast With Seven Heads

The third Scripture reference to an end-time empire which includes ten political leaders and their territories is found in Revelation 13:1, 2.

> And I stood upon the sand of the sea, and saw a beast rise up out of the sea, having seven heads and ten horns, and upon his horns ten crowns, and upon his heads the name of blasphemy.
> And the beast which I saw was like a leopard, and his feet were like the feet of a bear, and his mouth like the mouth of a lion; and the dragon gave him his power, and his throne, and great authority.

It is apparent that this vision of John has a striking similarity to the one we examined in Daniel 7, although the seven heads are something we did not see before. It is possible that these seven heads correspond to the seven kings of Revelation 17:10.

> And there are seven kings: five are fallen, and one is, and the other is not yet come; and when he cometh, he must continue a short space.

Three explanations of these seven heads are worthy of consideration.

1. They may refer to seven forms of government during different stages of Rome's history. When John wrote Revelation, five of them had appeared and disappeared in Roman history: kings, consuls, dictators, decemvirs, and military tribunals. The imperial form of government was in power. The seventh form of government would then be found for a brief time in the ten-nation confederacy that is still future. Whatever kind of government this will be, it will be abruptly changed when the "little horn," the blasphemous and arrogant world ruler, establishes an absolute dictatorship, causing all the world to marvel.

2. Some Bible scholars see these heads as representing seven successive Roman emperors; namely, Julius Caesar, Tiberius, Caligula, Claudius, Nero, Domitian, and the Antichrist making up the seventh one. They contend that the phrase, "even he is the eighth" (Revelation 17:11), indicates that he is a combination of all the features of the previous six.

3. Another explanation advanced is that the seven heads symbolize seven Gentile world powers which have manifested hostility against God's people. They list the empires as Egypt, Assyria, Babylon, Medo-Persia, Greece, Rome, and Diocletian's Quadripartate. The Antichrist's empire would be the eighth (Revelation 17:11).

In any case, the seven heads by no means contradict the clear assertion that the end-time political empire will involve ten nations in a confederacy.

Revelation 13 in a striking manner corroborates the prophecies made by Daniel. It confirms not only the ten-nation alliance, but also the time period of the world dictator's rule. Revelation 13:5 specifies that he will continue in power for forty-two months, which is precisely the same length of time that is indicated in Daniel 7:25.

THE HARLOT AND THE BEAST

We turn now to the fourth passage of Scripture which speaks of this future ten-nation alliance. It is Revelation 17 where we see the harlot riding upon the beast which has the seven heads and ten horns. This wicked woman represents the end-time union of religions in one organization. Her position on the beast indicates that for a time this religious system will exercise considerable influence upon the political empire while it protects her. This will not last very long, however. A sudden change will take place when the ten kingdoms, which are subservient to the beast, turn against the harlot and destroy her. The religious system which has played politics so cunningly will meet its end.

> And the ten horns which thou sawest upon the beast, these shall hate the harlot, and shall make her desolate and naked, and shall eat her flesh, and burn her with fire (Revelation 17:16).

This is in perfect conformity with what Revelation 13 tells us concerning the blasphemous political leader. He will not only speak against God and persecute the saints, but will also demand that all people worship him. Therefore, even the religious system represented by the harlot must be eliminated.

THE CLEAR PICTURE

The four Scripture passages we have examined clearly depict a future league of ten nations which will become subject to an extremely powerful and wicked man. They also describe the defeat of this political leader and his empire by the Son of Man, and portray the following establishment of His universal and everlasting kingdom.

What About the Roman Empire?

Many efforts have been made to identify the nations which will compose this end-time confederacy. The fact is, however, that the Scriptures nowhere give us this specific information. Nevertheless, we can conclude that this alliance will be made up of a Western bloc of powers. This ten-nation confederacy is definitely connected with the vision of Daniel 7, where the beast represents the historic Roman Empire. It is on this beast that the ten horns appear. We therefore must consider this alliance as the last stage of the Roman Empire. The objection is often raised that the Roman Empire is a thing of the past. It was divided into two sections by Theodosias in A.D. 395. The Western Empire ceased in A.D. 476, while the Eastern continued until 1453. However, though Rome did not continue in its imperial form as an empire, fragments have continued to exist as separate nations. Furthermore, Erich Sauer points out a number of indications that the Roman Empire never really died.

> Nevertheless from the lands which originally had been included in the Roman Empire there went out the most powerful, decisive impulses for the further development of the surviving civilized peoples of the sphere of this former Roman Empire. Only this fact enables us to understand why, in spite of all individual variations, and after the political collapse of Rome, Biblical prophecy views the consequent developments as connected with that empire, and sets it forth as one historical unity, even as being the one fourth world empire of Daniel continuing from the early Roman time to the end of the present age.
>
> The Roman administration lived on in the Church of Rome. The ecclesiastical provinces coincided with the State provinces; and Rome, the chief city of the world empire, became the chief city of the world Church, the seat of the Papacy.
>
> The Roman tongue lived on in the Latin of the Church, and is still in use in the international technical language of law, medicine, and natural science.

Roman law lived on in legislation. The corpus juris Romanum (body of Roman law) of the Eastern Roman Emperor Justinian (A.D. 527-565) became the foundation of jurisprudence among the Latin and Germanic peoples throughout the Middle Ages and far into modern times.

The Roman army lived on in military systems. It became the model for armaments and western defense. We still use Latin words such as captain, major, general, battalion, regiment, army, infantry, artillery, and cavalry.

Also the spirit of the Roman conception of the State has survived. It was marked by severest discipline, iron will, centralization, subordination of the individual to the community, devotion to the State, belief in its eternity, expressed in "eternal Rome" (Roma aeterna), idolization of the State, as in the Roman emperor cult, merging of the man in the citizen.

Finally, a certain mystery hovers around the history of the city of Rome itself:

about 1000 B.C.	— a poor village.
about A.D. 100	— a city of 1,000,000.
in the Middle Ages	— a medium-sized provincial town.
since the sixteenth century	— gradually increasing.
since 1870	— strong and rapid growth.
today	— again a million inhabitants as in the days of the Roman emperors.

Many of these facts are only historical incidents. Many of them appear for only a brief time and disappear. The value of observing them lies in this, that they enable us to perceive that, even after the collapse of Rome, in the subsequent development of the peoples of its area, and in the background of the whole process, there is at work a continuous, homogeneous, dynamic historical force which, in ever new forms, displays its permanence, vitality, and strength. This shows that in a wider sense the whole is actually one kingdom. At the same time this continuity, embracing centuries, becomes a sublime testimony to the reliability of the prophets and to their grasp of reality and to the accuracy of their historical foresight.[1]

---

[1]Sauer, Erich, *The Triumph of the Crucified,* (Grand Rapids: Eerdmans Pub. Co., 1952), pp. 132, 133. Used by permission.

THE OLD BORDERS?

Does this mean that the final form of the Roman Empire must exactly conform to the boundaries of the past? Certainly not! The boundaries of the Roman Empire varied from time to time. This is true of every great empire. Great Britain has remained Great Britain through hundreds of years of fluctuating borders. Even with a capital city other than Rome the coming ten-nation alliance could still be the Roman Empire.

A WESTERN POWER

The Roman Empire was definitely a western power. At the time of its greatest extent it covered western Europe, including England, along with the Middle East, embracing Egypt and North Africa. The influence of this great empire has been continued in the gradual westernization of the world. There is therefore good reason to believe that the ten kingdom alliance of the future will cover the geographical area of the old empire plus other nations and powers. It will be world-wide in influence and power according to Revelation 13:1-10. We cannot deny the possibility that the United States and other nations in our continent may be part of this end-time empire. The United States of America has aligned itself with the nations of western Europe. Some conclude that because the United States is not specifically named in the prophetic Scriptures it will be either completely destroyed or a second-rate power when this final confederacy of nations appears on the scene. This is not necessarily a correct deduction. It is quite possible, perhaps even probable, that the United States will play a significant role in the empire under the domination of Antichrist.

As we progress through this study we will see that Russia

is specifically named in the Old Testament and will definitely not be part of this alliance of nations. We will also note that the Far East becomes a source of concern to the world ruler of the end-time, and therefore must be excluded from this confederacy. All in all we have solid evidence that this revived Roman Empire is a western power. The present alignment of nations fits into the prophetic picture, and the formation of the common market in Europe may well have great significance.

Chapter Four

BRITISH-ISRAELISM EXAMINED

A theory that has received wide publicity sets forth the claim that the ten tribes, called Israel, are the Anglo-Saxon people, and that the present-day Jews represent the two tribes of Judah and Benjamin only. These theorists tell you that the ten tribes, after being taken into captivity, migrated to Great Britain, and that England and the United States are now Ephraim and Manasseh. This whole system of thought leads to utter confusion, and is hardly worthy of consideration. However, those who propound it claim that they have more than three million adherents, and are able to present a case for their position which on the surface looks quite plausible. Therefore, it is fitting that we examine some of the foundations upon which this speculative scheme is based.

An Erroneous Assumption

The whole concept rests upon the supposition that the ten tribes were lost. If it can be proven that this is not true, everything else the advocates of British-Israelism may say is of no avail to prove their case. The fact is that the ten tribes were never lost. The term "lost tribes" as applied to the ten tribes of Israel is a misnomer. It sounds wonderfully mysterious to talk about "lost tribes," and the idea that

51

perhaps they are members of God's chosen race proves very exciting to many people. This accounts for the popularity of this theory in some circles.

To prove that the ten tribes were never lost we need not go outside the Bible. We will not turn to mythological stories and legendary sources for our information as do the Anglo-Israel theorizers.

History of Israel and Judah

Most people who have some understanding of the Bible know that under Saul, David, and Solomon the people of Israel existed as twelve tribes, each with a territory of land assigned to it. The tribe of Levi was actually the thirteenth tribe, but it had no separate inheritance. (Two tribes came from Joseph through his sons Ephraim and Manasseh.) The kingdom suffered a split under Rehoboam, the son of Solomon. The ten northern tribes followed the leadership of Jeroboam who set himself up as their king in Tirzah (I Kings 14:17). Under Omri, the sixth king of the northern tribes, the capital city was moved to Samaria. This kingdom is variously designated as Israel, Samaria, and Ephraim in the Old Testament. It endured for around 250 years and was ruled by 19 wicked kings from 9 different families.

This northern kingdom engaged in the most depraved and degrading idolatrous worship throughout this entire period of time. Not one of the kings was a godly man, and the history of the royal families was filled with tragedy. The two tribes, on the other hand, retained the descendants of David as kings, and experienced three remarkable revivals of true religion. This southern kingdom continued for about 150 years after Israel went into captivity. Any study of the history of these two kingdoms indicates clearly that

Judah, not Israel, was the channel which God used to preserve the truth.

A Mistaken Concept

The British-Israel theory rests upon the idea that these two kingdoms existed as completely separate nations, and that they went on to absolutely distinct destinies. It does not allow for any mixture of its citizens, nor the possibility that all the people from the twelve tribes finally merged into one ethnic and religious group. The facts as recorded in the Old Testament, however, indicate that there was a constant intermingling of the people from the two kingdoms, and that after the captivity they gradually lost their tribal identity and finally were known everywhere as Jews.

All Did Not Leave the Southern Kingdom

Notice first that not all the people in the ten northern tribes followed Jeroboam when he established his separate kingdom. Some of the members of these tribes chose to unite with the people of Benjamin and Judah. This is clearly indicated in I Kings 12, verses 21-24. Rehoboam was tempted to use armed forces to break up Jeroboam's plan, but God told the prophet Shemaiah to forbid it.

> Speak unto Rehoboam, the son of Solomon, king of Judah, and unto all the house of Judah and Benjamin, *and to the remnant of the people,* saying,
> Thus saith the Lord, Ye shall not go up, nor fight against your brethren . . . (I Kings 12:23, 24).

This "remnant of the people" could be none other than individuals from the ten tribes who chose to remain with Rehoboam and the kingdom of Judah. It is apparent at the

very beginning that the southern kingdom actually represented people from all the tribes.

MANY RETURN TO JUDAH

As we progress through the historical records of the Old
Testament we find that the whole tribe of Levi joined the
southern kingdom, and a large number of the people from
the ten tribes who had originally left came back with these
Levites. II Chronicles 11:14-17 tells us:

> For the Levites left their suburban lands and their posses-
> sion, and came to Judah and Jerusalem; for Jeroboam and
> his sons had cast them off from executing the priest's office
> unto the Lord;
> And he appointed for himself priests for the high places,
> and for the he-goats, and for the calves which he had made.
> And after them, out of *all the tribes of Israel,* such as set
> their hearts to seek the Lord God of Israel came to Jerusalem,
> to sacrifice unto the Lord God of their fathers.
> So they strengthened the kingdom of Judah, and made
> Rehoboam, the son of Solomon, strong, three years; for three
> years they walked in the way of David and Solomon.

Apparently those who respected the true God returned to
the kingdom of David, which still had the temple and God's
prescribed worship ritual. Therefore, we once again see that
there was a gathering together of people from all the tribes
in the southern kingdom.

ANOTHER MULTITUDE RETURNS

A short time later, when under King Asa there was a
revival of true religion with obvious blessings from God in
the kingdom of Judah, a great number of the northern people united with their brethren to the south.

> And he gathered all Judah and Benjamin, and *the sojourners
> with them out of Ephraim and Manasseh, and out of Simeon;*

for they fell to him out of Israel in abundance, when they saw that the Lord, his God, was with him (II Chronicles 15:9).

Here a great number of the people from the ten tribes joined themselves to Asa and his people. It certainly is obvious that the kingdom of Judah did not represent only individuals from two tribes, but from all Israel as well.

STILL ANOTHER EXODUS FROM ISRAEL

Once again, under Hezekiah we find that the multitude who rejoiced together in the worship of God included the godly remnant from the ten tribes.

> And all the congregation of Judah, with the priests and the Levites, and *all the congregation who came out of Israel, and the sojourners who came out of the land of Israel,* and who dwelt in Judah, rejoiced.
> So there was great joy in Jerusalem; for since the time of Solomon, the son of David, king of Israel, there was not the like in Jerusalem (II Chronicles 30:25, 26).

These Scripture passages certainly show that the kingdom of Judah was the one that God recognized and favored, and that it was with this kingdom that the majority of the godly people from the ten tribes identified themselves. It was blessed with the dynasty of David, the temple of Solomon, and some godly kings who led it in revivals. The northern kingdom was without kings of God's choice, without God's prescribed worship, and without the temple God had designed.

GOD'S ESTIMATE OF JUDAH'S KINGS

God recognized the kings of Judah as the kings of His entire chosen nation. He never intended that the ten tribes should continue to exist as a separate kingdom, and He spoke of the day when the two kingdoms would be united in one, with Jerusalem as the center of worship and the capital city. In II Chronicles 21:1, 2, Jehoshaphat, the fourth king of the southern tribes, is called the *king of Israel.*

> Now Jehoshaphat slept with his fathers, and was buried with his fathers in the city of David. And Jehoram, his son, reigned in his stead.
> And he had brethren, the sons of Jehoshaphat: Azariah, and Jehiel, and Zechariah, and Azariah, and Michael, and Shephatiah; all these were the sons of *Jehoshaphat, king of Israel* (II Chronicles 21:1, 2).

In II Chronicles 28:19 Ahaz, the eleventh monarch in Judah, is called *king of Israel.*

God looked upon these descendants of David as the kings of His people, the entire twelve tribes. We have already pointed out that a good percentage of the inhabitants of Judah were indeed people from the ten tribes. The Lord apparently did not recognize the complete distinction between Israel and Judah that the Anglo-Israel theorists insist is an absolute necessity.

The Merging Continues

This is not the end of the merging process between the people from all the tribes, however. It continued even after the two kingdoms were taken into captivity. In 721 B.C. the ten tribes were defeated by the Assyrians and a number of them were taken captive. The Old Testament does not tell us how many of them were deported from their land, but an inscription by Sargon, who succeeded Shalmaneser when he died in 722 B.C., says, "I besieged the City of

Samaria, and took it. I carried off 27,280 of the citizens; I chose 50 chariots for myself from the whole number taken; all the other property of the people of the town I left for my servants to take. I appointed resident officers over them, and imposed on them the same tribute as had formerly been paid. In the place of those taken into captivity I sent thither inhabitants of lands conquered by me, and imposed the tribute on them which I required from Assyrians." It is possible that some other deportations took place, but this inscription indicates definitely that the vast majority of the people were left in their own territory under rulers appointed by Assyria. These citizens of the ten tribes continued to be the predominant population of the country, and many of them placed themselves under the rule of Judah. This is clearly pointed out by the fact that about 100 years after their defeat by Assyria and the deportation of some of the population, a great number of the people joined in the religious festivals during the revival under Josiah, king of Judah.

> And when they came to Hilkiah, the high priest, they delivered the money that was brought into the house of God, which the Levites who kept the doors had gathered of the hand of Manasseh and Ephraim, and of all the remnant of Israel, and of all Judah and Benjamin; and they returned to Jerusalem (II Chronicles 34:9). (See also II Chronicles 35: 17, 18.)

Thus we see that most of the people of the ten tribes were not uprooted by Assyria, but remained in their own territories and many voluntarily joined themselves to the king of Judah. In a very real sense, even after the ten tribes had been taken into captivity, the process of amalgamation between the people of Judah and Israel continued.

INTERMINGLING IN CAPTIVITY

Another mistake the Anglo-Israelites make in their effort to "lose" the ten tribes is that of overlooking the fact that Assyria and Babylon became virtually one empire. In fact, about 677 B.C., less than 50 years after the fall of Samaria, Esarhaddon ruled over both kingdoms. Therefore, when Babylon began to take captives out of Judah around 600 B.C. they were transported to precisely the same areas where the people from the ten tribes were living. It is not difficult to prove this. II Kings 17:6 tells us where the deported Israelites were taken, in about 721 B.C.

> In the ninth year of Hoshea, the king of Assyria took Samaria, and carried Israel away into Assyria, and placed them in *Halah* and in *Habor* by the river of *Gozan*, and in the cities of the Medes.

When Ezekiel was carried away to Babylon about 590 B.C., shortly before the complete defeat of Judah in 586 B.C., he and the other exiles from Judah lived in this territory. Ezekiel 1:1 declares, ". . . I was among the captives by the river of *Chebar*. . . ." A glance at the map of the Near East reveals that this was in Gozan, to the north, and not south near the city of Babylon. Consequently, these exiles from all the tribes of both the Assyrians and Babylonian captivities lived in the same areas. Here they gradually merged into one people.

REMNANT FROM ALL TRIBES

Some years later a remnant returned from captivity to the land of Palestine, and Ezra definitely recognized the Jews as representing all the tribes of Israel. This is clearly indicated in Ezra 6:17, "And offered at the dedication . . .

twelve he-goats, according to the number of the tribes of Israel."

All Became Known As Jews

When Alexander the Great came to power, many of the Jews settled in Palestine and enjoyed great freedom. Other Jews established colonies throughout the world of that day. Asia Minor, Cyprus, Crete, the coastal regions and islands of the Aegean Sea, southern Europe, Egypt, North Africa, even India and China, knew the presence of Jewish colonies. There were synagogues everywhere, but at the time of the great feast celebrations the city of Jerusalem was crowded with millions who came from far and near to express their loyalty to their faith. All those whose religion was connected with Moses, and who still looked to Jerusalem as the Holy City were considered to be Jews.

New Testament Recognizes Jews As Israelites

The ten tribes were not lost, and James recognized this when he wrote his epistle to the Jewish believers of his day. He saw them as representing the twelve tribes and used this very term in addressing them: ". . . to the *twelve tribes* which are scattered abroad, greeting" (James 1:1). In this day when anti-Semitism once again rears its ugly head, let us remember that every one of the apostles whom the Lord Jesus chose was loyal to the religion centered in Jerusalem around the temple. Jesus Christ Himself participated in the ceremonies of this Jewish faith. When He sent His apostles to the lost sheep of the house of Israel, these lost persons were obviously Jews. According to the Anglo-Israelites the true Israelites had now been established in Great Britain for several hundred years. The Lord

Jesus apparently did not know this, for He sent His apostles throughout the land of Judaea to reach these lost sheep of the house of Israel. It was to the synagogues that Jesus and His apostles went to carry on their ministry. Remember, too, that on the day of Pentecost great multitudes of people from every part of the Roman Empire who adhered to the Jewish faith gathered for their religious holidays. The people to whom Peter preached on the day of Pentecost were the same ones who had cried, "Crucify Him, Crucify Him. His blood be on us and our children." Listen to Peter's declaration to them,

> *Ye men of Israel*, hear these words: Jesus of Nazareth, a man approved of God among you by miracles and wonders and signs, which God did by him in the midst of you, as ye yourselves also know;
> Him, being delivered by the determinate counsel and fore-knowledge of God, ye have taken, and by wicked hands have crucified and slain;
> Whom God hath raised up, having loosed the pains of death, because it was not possible that he should be holden of it (Acts 2:22-24).

These same people who had rejected Christ were the ones to whom Peter gave the message of repentance. He promised that if they would turn to Christ their sins would be blotted out and the times of refreshing promised by the Old Testament prophets would become a reality. In other words, Peter told these same Jews who had crucified the Lord Jesus that this Christ would return as their King if they would receive Him.

> Repent, therefore, and be converted, that your sins may be blotted out, when the times of refreshing shall come from the presence of the Lord;
> And he shall send Jesus Christ, who before was preached unto you,

Whom the heaven must receive until the times of restitution of all things, which God hath spoken by the mouth of all his holy prophets since the age began.

For Moses truly said unto the fathers, A prophet shall the Lord, your God, raise up unto you of your brethren, like unto me; him shall ye hear in all things, whatever he shall say unto you.

And it shall come to pass that every soul, who will not hear that prophet, shall be destroyed from among the people.

Yea, and all the prophets from Samuel and those who follow after, as many as have spoken, have likewise foretold of these days.

Ye are the sons of the prophets, and of the covenant which God made with our fathers, saying unto Abraham, And in thy seed shall all the kindreds of the earth be blessed.

Unto you first God, having raised up his Son, Jesus, sent him to bless you, in turning away every one of you from his iniquities (Acts 3:19-26).

If the Anglo-Israelites be right in their assertion that the true Israelites, the inheritors of the promises, were now quite well established in the area of Great Britain, then Peter made a terrible mistake in this message to the Jews who had rejected Jesus Christ.

Having established that the ten tribes were never lost, and that the Jews today represent all the tribes of Israel, we would like to consider briefly some of the grounds upon which the British-Israel proponents base their teaching.

BASED ON LEGENDS

One would expect that a theory of this nature would be built upon a great deal of historical material. This is not the case, however. These theorists contend that some of the members of the lost tribes made their way toward Denmark, and from Denmark some went on to England. They say that another group from the tribe of Dan followed Jeremiah to Ireland in the sixth century B.C., among them

Tea Tephi, who they claim was the daughter of Zedekiah, the last king of Judah. She fell in love with Heremon, king of Ireland, and they were married. They then present a list of names to indicate that Queen Victoria is a descendant of this pair, and that through this alleged daughter of Zedekiah the throne of David was transferred from Jerusalem to Great Britain. As historical evidence from the Bible the best they can produce is a reference to some daughters of the king of Judah who were taken into Egypt (Jeremiah 41:10; 43:6). There is positively no evidence that Zedekiah had a daughter who ever went to Ireland. Nor do we have any real reason to believe there ever was a person by the name of Tea Tephi. A few of the ancient ballads speak of an Irish Queen named Tea and others mention a British Queen by the name of Tephi. All of this is part of the ancient folklore of Great Britain and cannot be considered history. The Anglo-Israelites manage to bring these names of two mythical persons together to refer to one person, a daughter of Zedekiah.

ENDLESS GENEALOGIES

As one reads the literature produced by the Anglo-Israelites to establish a genealogy that extends from Adam to the present rulers of Great Britain, the inspired words of the Apostle Paul come to mind. He exhorted young Timothy,

> Neither give heed to fables and endless genealogies, which minister questions rather than godly edifying which is in faith . . . (I Timothy 1:4).

THRONE-RIGHT NOT THROUGH ZEDEKIAH

One is almost inclined to view this theory with good-natured amusement. It is a well-known fact that there is no reliable Irish history until several centuries after Christ.

No respectable scholar will for a moment take seriously these ludicrous claims of the Anglo-Israel theorizers. We wonder why the British-Israelites never make reference to the fact that Zedekiah was not even a rightful king of Judah. He was made king by Nebuchadnezzar, but did not have the legal right to the throne. He was an uncle of the last legal king; namely, Jehoiachin (II Kings 24:17, 18), whose sons were heir to the throne (I Chronicles 3:17, 18; Matthew 1:11, 12). Even if Zedekiah had had surviving sons, they would not have been legal heirs to the throne.

In fact, it is obvious from the Scriptures that although he reigned as king for a time, God never recognized Zedekiah as such. Matthew does not even name him in his genealogy, and follows the family of Jehoiachin in establishing the legal right of Jesus Christ to the Throne of David (see Matthew 1:1-17). In Ezekiel 12, verses 1-20, the approaching conquest of Jerusalem is foretold, and in verse 12 the prophet pictures Zedekiah as leaving almost everything behind and entering into bondage. Ezekiel predicted that he would not even see the land where he was going, and this was fulfilled when the Babylonians, after killing his sons in his sight, removed his eyes. Thus blinded, Zedekiah died in the unseen land of his captors. You will notice that as Ezekiel by inspiration referred to Zedekiah he did not call him the king of Israel. He referred to him as "the prince in Jerusalem."

> Say thou unto them, Thus saith the Lord God: This burden concerneth the *prince in Jerusalem,* and all the house of Israel that are among them (Ezekiel 12:10).

God's Curse on Jehoiachin

The Anglo-Israelites sometimes point out that God pronounced a curse upon Jehoiachin (Jeremiah 22:24-30), and that therefore the throne-right passed to his uncle Zedekiah. This is not true, however. Although the curse upon Jehoiachin's seed would indeed eliminate his literal descendants from actual possession of the throne, Jesus was not a physical descendant of Jehoiachin. Matthew in the first chapter of his gospel was establishing our Lord's legal right to the Throne of David. As the adopted son of Joseph, the curse upon Jehoiachin's seed did not apply to Him. Moreover, Zedekiah is in no manner recognized as an ancestor of Jesus Christ in any of the New Testament genealogies. It is bad enough to latch hold of ancient and contradictory myths to establish a theory, but it is a double insult to our intelligence to ask that we accept the transfer of the Throne of David from Jerusalem to Great Britain through a mythical *female* descendant of a man who had no right to the throne in the first place.

CHILDISH PLAY ON WORD SOUNDS

Another method used by these speculators to bolster their theory is the reading of great significance into similar sounds in words. Because the Hebrew word "berith" means "covenant," and the Hebrew "ish" means "man," they conclude that "British" means "men of covenant." They do not seem much impressed by the fact that philologists are unanimous in declaring that there is no connection between the Hebrew language and the Anglo-Saxon tongue.

This is what Dr. Lawrence Duff-Forbes has to say about the claim that "British" means "men of the covenant":

> But hold! There is a fly in the ointment! Since the word "covenant" possesses no adjectival force in Hebrew, the two nouns are in what is known as the construct state. So placed, the meaning would be "a man of a covenant," but even for this concept it should rather be "Ish HaBrith." Thus, to get

even remotely near this philological monstrosity we would require to reverse the order of the words.

The B/I (British-Israel) balderdash based on "Brit-ish," if it proves anything proves too much. For what of the word "BRITAIN"? Permitting me a similar use of assonance, may I remark that "Ain" in Hebrew is a particle of negation, meaning "NOT" or "WITHOUT." It is so translated in Hosea 3:4, "AIN MELECK," "without a king," etc. Thus, if "BRIT-ISH" is "COVENANT-MAN," then "BRIT-AIN" is "WITHOUT A COVENANT!"

Professor U. H. Parker, professor of Hebrew at McMaster University, Hamilton, Ont., has already pointed out the unscholarly gasconade of British-Israelism in this direction. Of the words, "British" and "Britain," he says: "These words are not Hebrew, nor has any Hebrew scholar ever supposed them to be such. 'Britain' is an ancient Celtic or West-Germanic term. It appears, in its cognate form, in the classics, and was handed down to modern England via both Old English and Latin. Incidentally, it is really the plural of 'Briton.' 'British' is simply the old Celtic 'Bret' (a Briton) plus the familiar suffix 'ish,' which is used to form adjectives of common Teutonic origin. This suffix is cognate with the German 'isc,' the Dutch 'isch' and the Greek 'iskos.' To persist, as some do, in seeking to identify it with the Hebrew word 'eesh' (man) might well be described as mulish, childish, and foolish.

British-Israelites do considerable violence to philology generally. They weave a fanciful tale that "Isaac's sons" is really the basis of the word "SAXONS." The·full humor of this can only be appreciated by a Hebrew scholar! If it is really legitimate to thus ride from one nationality to another by saddling an assonance, could we not equally prove that the inhabitants of Hamburg were mountaineers of negro origin violating the Jewish dietary laws? Again warning against the vagaries of B/I, Professor Parker declares: "As a matter of fact there are hardly more than two dozen words, exclusive of Bible names, in the English vocabulary which can be traced to Hebrew roots. . . . Nearly every one of the "Hebrew" words we do have come to us via the Greeks, and might more reasonably be credited to Phoenician than to Hebrew."[1]

---

[1]Duff-Forbes, Lawrence, *The Baleful Bubble of "British-Israelism,"* (Whittier: Dr. Lawrence Duff-Forbes, 1961), pp. 32, 33. Used by permission.

THE TRAIL OF DAN

We could give many examples of this kind of pseudo-scholarship among the proponents of the British-Israel view, but one more will suffice. To follow the movements of the tribe of Dan and to prove that it was among those that settled in Ireland, they point to the many instances that a "din," "dun," or "don" is part of the name of a territory, city, or river where they supposedly passed through or settled. A few of the names mentioned are: Mace*don*ia, Dar*dan*elles, *Dan*ube, *Den*mark, *Dun*bar, Lon*don*, etc. However, several students have pointed out that using this same kind of reasoning we could establish that the tribe of Dan went to Africa where are the *Dan*akil and *Din*ka tribes, where the *Don*alists are a Christian cult, and where one can find *Don*do, and *Den*kera. Any imaginative person could present a wonderful case for the settling of each of the tribes in areas all over the world if he does with their names what the Anglo-Israelites do with Dan.

A PROBLEM FOR BRITISH-ISRAELISM

Many other factors make positive our assertion that Great Britain and the United States cannot be Ephraim and Manasseh. We know that Jacob and his sons were in the line of Shem. The mates they chose were Hamitic (even Joseph, by marrying an Egyptian girl, produced offspring that was Semitic-Hamitic). If the Tarshish of Ezekiel 38 is Britain, as the Anglo-Israelites claim, then its people must be Japhetic. Genesis 10:4 makes it clear that Tarshish is a descendant of Japheth. Thus the identification of Britain as Tarshish makes absolutely impossible the claim that its inhabitants are Ephraimites.

A Voyage That Worked Wonders

It is also rather amusing to find the United States designated as Manasseh. Its people come from every part of the world. If the Anglo-Israelites insist that the early citizens (not the Indians) are people of Manasseh, one cannot help but wonder how the ocean voyage worked this miraculous change. The people who left England walked on the ship Ephraimites and left it Manassehites. One writer wonders if the sea air had the strange potency to make this transformation.

No Hebrew Traces in British History

It is also interesting to note that Hebrew writing is from right to left while all writing in Britain has always been left to right. Furthermore, not one bit of early British history reveals any traces of the Hebrew religion. It is well known that the ten tribes as a kingdom never worshiped the true God, but one would expect some evidence of their former contact with the Law of Moses. However, the early inhabitants of Britain were thoroughly pagan.

The Stone of Scone

From time to time you will hear some fantastic claims made for the Stone of Scone, the stone under the coronation throne in Westminster Abbey where the Kings and Queens of England are crowned. Legend has it that this stone, which once resided in the famous Abbey in Scone, a village of Scotland, is the stone Jacob used for a pillow when he fled from his brother Esau. A very extensive mythology has been built up in connection with this stone. It is reported that this is the stone from which Moses secured water, and that it followed the Israelites wherever they went. The

British-Israelites connect it with many of the historical incidents in the Bible where different kinds of stones, rocks, and pillars are mentioned. It matters very little to them that completely different Hebrew words are used to indicate these various types of rocks or stones.

Legendary, Not Historical

The Coronation Stone is a dull reddish or purplish sandstone with a few pebbles embedded in it, and there is complete agreement among geologists that no stone like this could possibly have come from the land of Palestine. Furthermore, scientists who have analyzed the Stone of Scone have found it to be definitely of Scottish origin. The nation of England keeps this stone because of tradition. The leading people in England are well aware of the legendary nature of the reports concerning its history, but retain it merely as a symbol. In any case, the idea that it is kept because the leaders of Great Britain are the seed royal to the house of David must be dismissed as too ridiculous for serious consideration. At least six different "houses" have been crowned over this stone since it was taken from the Scots in 1296 and brought to England. It is amazing that in this enlightened day many people would still put stock in the fantastic and unhistorical legends connected with this stone.

The Davidic Covenant

It may be that you recognize the fallacy of the British-Israel conjecture, but wonder about God's promise to David concerning the perpetuity of his house and throne. God's unconditional covenant with David is recorded in II Samuel 7:12-16,

> And when thy days be fulfilled, and thou shalt sleep with thy fathers, I will set up thy seed after thee, which shall proceed out of thine own body, and I will establish his kingdom.
>
> He shall build an house for my name, and I will establish the throne of his kingdom forever.
>
> I will be his father, and he shall be my son, If he commit iniquity, I will chasten him with the rod of men, and with the stripes of the children of men;
>
> But my mercy shall not depart away from him, as I took it from Saul, whom I put away before thee.
>
> And thine house and thy kingdom shall be established forever before thee; thy throne shall be established forever.

This covenant assured David that his successor would be one of his own sons, that this son would build the temple, and that God would never take the kingship of Israel from his family as He had done in the case of Saul. David's house, his throne and his kingdom will endure forever. These promises are restated and confirmed in later Scriptures.

We know there has been no rightful king of David's line since Jehoiachin. (Remember that Zedekiah was put in authority by Nebuchadnezzar, and Ezekiel referred to him not as king, but prince. Moreover, Matthew 1:11 records Jeconiah, who is Jehoiachin, as the last king of Judah. God did show some mercy to Zedekiah, in that he was not slaughtered by Nebuchadnezzar, and he received an honorable burial upon his death, according to Jeremiah 34:2-5. However, this in no way indicates that God recognized him as a rightful heir to the throne.)

God Promised Chastisement for Disobedience

What about God's covenant with David? Has God failed to do what He said He would? We already know that the myth which declares that the kingdom of David was transferred to Great Britain through a daughter of Zedekiah is an impossible solution to our problem. The answer must be found in a proper understanding of the promises God made to David. God did not tell him that his descendants would reign upon the throne without a break. He warned David that when these heirs of the throne disobeyed Him they would be chastened. Historically, this was first fulfilled when the kingdom was divided, and then more fully when the Babylonians conquered Judah in 586 B.C. However, though the nation and her kings sinned, and therefore had to suffer a time during which there was no actual throne and kingdom, God has given assurance that He will always preserve a lineage with a right to the throne, and that David's kingdom was eternally established. David's house will yet literally take up the reins of government of this kingdom which was "established forever."

THE TESTIMONY OF PSALM 89

Psalm 89 is a powerful prophetic declaration that God will someday fulfill every pledge made to David even though for a time it may seem as if these promises have been canceled. The Psalmist declares the absolute certainty of God's Word in verses 27-38:

> Also I will make him my firstborn, higher than the kings of the earth.
> My mercy will I keep for him for evermore, and my covenant shall stand fast with him.
> His seed also will I make to endure forever, and his throne as the days of heaven.
> If his children forsake my law, and walk not in mine ordinances;
> If they break my statutes, and keep not my commandments;
> Then will I visit their transgression with the rod, and their iniquity with stripes.

> Nevertheless, my loving-kindness will I not utterly take from him, nor allow my faithfulness to fail.
>
> My covenant will I not break, nor will I alter the thing that is gone out of my lips.
>
> Once have I sworn by my holiness that I will not lie unto David.
>
> His seed shall endure forever, and his throne as the sun before me.
>
> It shall be established forever like the moon, and as a faithful witness in heaven. Selah.
>
> But thou hast cast off and abhorred, thou hast been angry with thine anointed.

The Psalmist then contemplates the apparent situation after Judah was taken into captivity. It *appeared* as if God had forgotten His promises, which of course is something God cannot do.

> Thou hast made void the covenant of thy servant; thou hast profaned his crown by casting it to the ground.
>
> Thou hast made his glory to cease, and cast his throne down to the ground (Psalm 89:39, 44).

What God Promised David

God never promised David that his descendants in unbroken succession would sit upon the throne, but He did give him His word that He would preserve a royal seed and a kingdom which would be established forever, and build up his throne to all generations (Psalm 89:4). God did not say, "*through* all succeeding generations without interruption." Thus, Jeremiah, in days of evil and approaching calamity, declared that God would someday bring about blessing to Israel and the world through a righteous king from the seed of David.

> Behold, the days come, saith the Lord, that I will perform that good thing which I have promised unto the house of Israel and to the house of Judah.

> In those days, and at that time, will I cause the Branch of righteousness to grow up unto David; and he shall execute justice and righteousness in the land.
>
> In those days shall Judah be saved, and Jerusalem shall dwell safely; and this is the name by which she shall be called, *the Lord, our righteousness*.
>
> For thus saith the Lord, David shall never lack a man to sit upon the throne of the house of Israel (Jeremiah 33:14-17).

The promise that there will always be a man to sit on David's Throne is not a declaration that every generation will see a son of David reigning on the earth, but an assurance that God will preserve David's lineage so that it is unbroken down through the centuries.

Hosea's Prophecy

The prophet Hosea also predicted that for a time the house of David would not possess a literal throne and rule over Israel.

> For the children of Israel shall abide many days without a king, and without a prince, and without a sacrifice, and without an image, and without an ephod, and without teraphim;
>
> Afterward shall the children of Israel return, and seek the Lord, their God, and David, their king, and shall fear the Lord and his goodness in the latter days (Hosea 3:4, 5).

This prophecy is meaningless and, in fact, untrue if the Throne of David was transferred to Great Britain in the manner suggested by the British-Israelites. If the throne was almost immediately transported to Great Britain through Zedekiah's daughter, then Israel did not "abide many days without a king."

What Did Jesus Say?

One more objection to the teaching that the Jews as a nation will inherit great spiritual and material blessing in the millennial age deserves our attention. The words of the Lord Jesus as recorded in Matthew 21:43 are often misunderstood.

> Therefore say I unto you, The kingdom of God shall be taken from you, and given to a nation bringing forth the fruits of it.

Many believe this text is an affirmation that the kingdom will be taken from the Jews and given as a permanent possession to another nation. If Jesus meant this, however, He would have contradicted many of the plain declarations of the Old Testament, and would make erroneous the assertion of Paul in Romans 11:25. Paul definitely affirmed that the nation of Israel will once again return to the center of God's program at the close of the present age. Therefore, it is well to take note of the fact that Jesus here used a term not often found in Matthew. He spoke of the "kingdom of God," the sphere of genuine possession, in contrast to the usual "kingdom of heaven," the sphere of profession. Jesus told these unbelieving scribes and Pharisees that because they rejected Him they would not be saved. Instead, the Gospel would go to a nation that would bring forth the fruits of salvation. The Church of the present age is that nation. Speaking of the Church, in a context where he quoted from Psalm 118:22, 23, even as Jesus did on this occasion, Peter declared,

> But ye are a chosen generation, a royal priesthood, *an holy nation,* a people of his own, that ye should show forth the praises of him who hath called you out of darkness into his marvelous light (I Peter 2:9).

The reference to another nation is not, therefore, an indication that some earthly nation other than Israel shall now inherit the physical blessing promised to the seed of Abraham through Isaac.

It is also well to recognize that the Lord was speaking to the chief priests and elders, the civil and religious leaders of that time who were determined to destroy Him. The people on the previous day had actually acclaimed Him as the "Son of David" (Matthew 21:45, 46), so that He was not addressing the people in general, but the leaders who were so intent upon His destruction. The chief priests and Pharisees knew that Jesus was speaking of them, not of the nation as a whole, because we are told in Matthew 21:45, "And when the chief priests and Pharisees had heard his parables, they perceived that he *spoke of them.*" Though these particular Jewish leaders were thus excluded from the kingdom of God, individual Jews can still be saved today if they trust Christ as Savior. And then we know that Israel as a nation will also still realize the blessings God has promised. Even as only a renewed people today enter the kingdom of God in the Church, so in the millennial age, the Jewish nation to whom the kingdom will be given will be a new nation spiritually, though it will also still be the same nation historically which came down through Abraham, Isaac, Jacob and his sons.

The Jews living upon earth today are the Israelites. They are the people to whom God has made many great and glorious promises. They will someday turn to God, inherit all the blessings that God has promised, and be revered among the nations.

Chapter Five

THE LAND OF CANAAN

The unrest and ferment found in the land of Palestine in these modern days is nothing new to that region. It is, rather, a continuation of the strife which for centuries has characterized that particular portion of the globe. Many wars have been waged, and much blood has been shed as the armies of succeeding generations have battled again and again for possession of the same parched, barren and bleak areas.

Not only are the nations of earth interested in the Middle East, but that part of the world has always had and continues to have a very unique position in God's program and purposes. This area is the cradle of human civilization. Adam and Eve were placed by God in the Garden of Eden located near the Euphrates River (Genesis 2:14).

LAND OF ABRAHAM

It was to Canaan that God called Abraham when He commanded him to leave his father's house. Genesis 12:1-3 tells us,

> . . . the Lord had said unto Abram, Get thee out of thy country, and from thy kindred, and from thy father's house, unto a land that I will show thee;

> And I will make of thee a great nation, and I will bless
> thee, and make thy name great; and thou shalt be a blessing.
> And I will bless them that bless thee, and curse him that
> curseth thee: and in thee shall all families of the earth be
> blessed.

Although the land of Canaan was not specifically named by God in this promise, Abraham knew this was where the Lord wanted him to go for verse 5 declares that ". . . they went forth to go into the land of Canaan; and into the land of Canaan they came" (Genesis 12:5).

It was to the descendants of Abraham that God gave the entire land from the River Nile in Egypt northward to the River Euphrates. Bounded by the Mediterranean Sea, this is an area of some 250,000 square miles. It includes most of the Sinai Peninsula, Edom, Transjordan, Negev, Syria, and in general the areas occupied by the Arabian nations. We read in Genesis 15:18, "In the same day the Lord made a covenant with Abram, saying, Unto thy seed have I given this land, from the river of Egypt unto the great river, the river Euphrates."

(Some interpreters look upon this "river of Egypt" as the Wadi el 'Arish, a small stream in the Sinai Peninsula. It seems a bit unlikely that this insignificant winter torrent should be set in juxtaposition to the great Euphrates.)

This is the only area upon earth thus given by God to a certain people long before they actually became a nation.

In addition to this, the Lord specified which one of Abraham's sons should be the heir of this portion of land. He said: ". . . in Isaac shall thy seed be called" (Genesis 21:12).

The descendants of Abraham through Isaac are the rightful owners of the entire land of Canaan.

LAND OF UNCONDITIONAL PROMISE

We also find that this land was given by God to Abraham's seed without any strings attached. The unconditional nature of this gift is clearly declared in Genesis 17, verses 7 and 8, where the Lord said:

> . . . I will establish my covenant between me and thee and thy seed after thee in their generations for an everlasting covenant, to be a God unto thee, and to thy seed after thee.
> And I will give unto thee, and to thy seed after thee, the land wherein thou are a sojourner, all the land of Canaan, for an everlasting possession; and I will be their God.

LAND OF PROPHETIC PRONOUNCEMENT

When the Lord, some 400 years after Abraham, gave Israel its constitution at Mt. Sinai, He predicted that the people would disobey Him, and that they would be driven out of Canaan and scattered among the nations. Verses 32 and 33 of Leviticus 26 record God's word concerning this. He said:

> And I will bring the land [Canaan] into desolation: and your enemies who dwell therein shall be astonished at it.
> And I will scatter you among the nations, and will draw out a sword after you; and your land shall be desolate, and your cities waste.

History stands as proof of the literal fulfillment of this prophecy. In 721 B.C. the northern ten tribes were carried away into captivity by Assyria. About 140 years later in 586 B.C., the southern two tribes were taken into Babylon. Seventy years later a handful of about 40,000 returned under Zerubbabel, Ezra and Nehemiah, but all the rest were scattered to the four corners of the earth. In A.D. 70 under Titus the Roman, Jerusalem was utterly destroyed and the remnant dispersed among the nations. Bible prophecy has

a great deal to say about other countries, but only of Canaan
do we find such a complete and entire history so minutely
foretold.

Land Where Jesus Walked

It was in Canaan that Jesus Christ was born, lived, died,
and arose from the grave. It was from this land that the
preaching of the Gospel went out to all the earth. To a
handful of Jewish believers in the city of Jerusalem the Lord
Jesus declared:

> But ye shall receive power, after that the Holy Ghost is
> come upon you; and ye shall be witnesses unto me both in
> Jerusalem, and in all Judaea, and in Samaria, and unto the
> uttermost part of the earth (Acts 1:8).

The glorious message of redemption, the Gospel of the
Lord Jesus Christ, had its beginning in this area of the
world.

Land of Israel's Restoration

The significance of the land of Palestine did not end,
however, with the ascension of Jesus Christ, nor even with
the destruction of Jerusalem in A.D. 70. God is not finished
with the Jewish nation, nor with the land which He gave
them to possess fully. One of the greatest miracles of all the
ages has been the preservation of the Jews in fulfillment of
God's promise found in Leviticus 26, verses 44 and 45. The
Lord said:

> And yet for all that, when they are in the land of their
> enemies, I will not cast them away, neither will I abhor them,
> to destroy them utterly, and to break my covenant with them;
> for I am the Lord their God.
>
> But I will for their sakes remember the covenant of their
> ancestors, whom I brought forth out of Egypt in the sight of
> the nations, that I might be their God: I am the Lord.

Today, after centuries of catastrophic judgments there are more than twice as many Jews as in the most splendid days of David and Solomon. This is amazing when we consider that one million one hundred thousand Jews were killed by Titus in A.D. 70, and that for 1800 years the Jews were homeless and bitterly persecuted. In addition to this, our own generation has witnessed the brutal massacre of some six million of them under Hitler. The fact that there are Jews today is a miracle in itself. Other peoples living under such extreme circumstances would long ago have lost their identity. Their very existence in the state of Israel today makes this a double miracle that is absolutely without parallel among the nations. The words of God in Isaiah 66:22 have been fulfilled: "For as the new heavens and the new earth, which I will make, shall remain before me, saith the Lord, so shall your seed and your name remain."

In the light of the prophetic Scriptures, the presence of the Jews in Palestine today is of tremendous significance, even though they have returned to the land in unbelief. According to Ezekiel 36, verses 24 through 28, it is *after* the return of a remnant that the nation of Israel will be converted to Jesus Christ, and begin to live for God's glory. Here are the Lord's own words as recorded in Ezekiel 36 and directed to God's chosen people:

> For I will take you from among the nations, and gather you out of all countries, and will bring you into your own land.
> *Then* will I sprinkle clean water upon you, and ye shall be clean. . . .
> A new heart also will I give you. . . .
> And ye shall dwell in the land that I gave to your fathers; and ye shall be my people, and I will be your God (Ezekiel 36:24-26, 28).

Moreover, in Ezekiel's vision of the dry bones (Ezekiel 37:1-14) the bones are brought together and are clothed with flesh *before* they receive the breath of life. The re-gathering of Israel in unbelief, then, is a necessary condition for the complete fulfillment of prophecy.

LAND OF RUSSIA'S OVERTHROW

The land of Palestine also holds a unique place in God's program since it is here that the final overthrow of the armies of Russia will take place. Ezekiel, chapters 38 and 39, give a vivid description of its supernatural and crushing defeat. That this passage of Scripture deals with Russia is clear both from linguistic considerations and from the geographical location of that country as the great power directly to the north of Palestine. When Israel shall be dwelling in peace and safety, feeling completely secure, then Russia will come down upon the land. The prophet Ezekiel records God's prediction of that day with these words,

> And thou shalt say, I will go up to the land of unwalled villages; I will go to those who are at rest, who dwell safely, all of them dwelling without walls, and having neither bars nor gates,
>
> To take a spoil, and to take a prey; to turn thine hand upon the desolate places that are now inhabited, and upon the people that are gathered out of the nations, who have gotten cattle and goods, who dwell in the midst of the land.
>
> And thou shalt come up against my people of Israel, like a cloud to cover the land; it shall be in the latter days, and I will bring thee against my land, that the nations may know me, when I shall be sanctified in thee, O Gog, before their eyes (Ezekiel 38:11, 12, 16).

The rest of this chapter and a large part of chapter 39 describe the defeat of these armies from the north. Ezekiel places the fulfillment of this prophecy in "the latter years" and "the latter days" (38:8, 16). The time is further specified as coming before the final regathering and conversion of Israel (Ezekiel 39:22-29).

LAND OF ANTICHRIST'S FINAL DEFEAT

Another reason God is vitally interested in the land of Palestine is that this area will play an important part in the career of the Antichrist, the coming political world ruler. In Daniel 9:27 we are told that this dictator will make a seven-year pact with those Jews who are in the land of Israel at the time of his accession to power. In the middle of this seven-year period he shall deliberately break this treaty and inaugurate an intense persecution of the Jewish people, which will precipitate the most dreadful time in their troubled history. Here is the exact account as given in Daniel 9,

> And he [the coming Roman Prince] shall confirm the covenant with many for one week; and in the midst of the week he shall cause the sacrifice and the oblation to cease, and for the overspreading of abominations he shall make it desolate, even until the consummation, and that determined shall be poured upon the desolate (Daniel 9:27).

The Battle of Armageddon, in which the Antichrist meets his final defeat, will also be fought in the land of Canaan. This battle is described in Zechariah 14 and Revelation 19.

LAND OF MESSIAH'S REIGN

When Jesus Christ comes in power and glory to destroy the enemies and to establish His Kingdom, it is upon the Mount of Olives that His feet shall stand (Zechariah 14:4). He will then bring peace, justice and prosperity to this weary world.

The city from which the Lord shall rule will be Jerusalem.
Isaiah tells us:

> . . . for out of Zion shall go forth the law, and the word
> of the Lord from Jerusalem.
>
> And he shall judge among the nations, and shall rebuke
> many peoples; and they shall beat their swords into plowshares,
> and their spears into pruning hooks; nation shall not lift up
> sword against nation, neither shall they learn war any more
> (Isaiah 2:3, 4).

The land of Canaan, its capital city, and the nation of
Israel are indeed precious in God's sight. In fact, the Lord
has given both a promise and a warning in relation to Israel.
He said: "And I will bless them that bless thee, and curse
him that curseth thee . . ." (Genesis 12:3).

The prophet Zechariah, declaring God's love for the historic people of Israel and their beloved city of Jerusalem,
said, ". . . he that toucheth you toucheth the apple of his
eye" (Zechariah 2:8).

Godly people the world over should "Pray for the peace
of Jerusalem" (Psalm 122:6). When we do so, we are in
reality praying for our Lord's return since Jerusalem and the
world will never experience true peace until Jesus Christ
comes again as the Prince of Peace.

> . . . Even so, come, Lord Jesus (Revelation 22:20).

Chapter Six

ISRAEL'S SEVENTY WEEKS

One of the key passages to a proper understanding of Bible prophecy and the future of Israel is found in Daniel, chapter 9. A correct interpretation of this portion of God's Word is a key which will unlock many other prophetic pronouncements.

> Seventy weeks are determined upon thy people and upon thy holy city, to finish the transgression, and to make an end of sins, and to make reconciliation for iniquity, and to bring in everlasting righteousness, and to seal up the vision and prophecy, and to anoint the most Holy.
>
> Know, therefore, and understand, that from the going forth of the commandment to restore and to build Jerusalem unto the Messiah, the Prince, shall be seven weeks, and threescore and two weeks; the street shall be built again, and the wall, even in troublous times.
>
> And after threescore and two weeks shall Messiah be cut off, but not for himself; and the people of the prince that shall come shall destroy the city and the sanctuary, and the end of it shall be with a flood, and unto the end of the war desolations are determined.
>
> And he shall confirm the covenant with many for one week; and in the midst of the week he shall cause the sacrifice and the oblation to cease, and for the overspreading of abominations he shall make it desolate, even until the consummation, and that determined shall be poured upon the desolate (Daniel 9:24-27).

490 YEARS FOR THE JEWS

Notice first of all that the predictions in these verses concern the Jews and the city of Jerusalem. Daniel tells us, "Seventy weeks are determined upon *thy people* and upon *thy holy city* . . ." (Daniel 9:24).

Since Daniel was a Jew, and the holy city Jerusalem, we must of necessity apply that which follows to Israel. This does not have reference to the Church.

Bearing in mind that these predictions concern Israel, let us analyze the significance and real meaning of some of the key phrases in verse 24, all pointing forward to some wonderful blessings awaiting God's chosen people. There are six statements in this verse which foretell some of the glory awaiting them.

1. The declaration that "Seventy weeks are determined . . . to finish the transgression," means precisely what it says in our English versions. The Hebrew word *kala* translated "finish," means "to complete." For that reason it would be erroneous to render this phrase, "to *atone* for transgressions." Daniel had been confessing the sins of Israel, and is assured by God that the time will come when they shall no longer live in disobedience to Him.

2. The phrase "to make an end of sins" declares that sin will be brought under complete control. In Job 37:7 the Hebrew word translated "make an end of" is rendered as "He sealeth up." Sin will be brought under full restraint of Divine government.

3. The expression "to make reconciliation for iniquity" refers to the effective realization of the reconciliation the Lord Jesus wrought at Calvary. This will take place when Israel as a nation turns to Jesus Christ in faith.

4. "To bring in everlasting righteousness" also expresses a promise which awaits Israel's conversion and will be experienced under the righteous rule of the Messiah.

5. The assertion that seventy weeks are determined "to seal up the vision and prophecy" obviously points to something still future. Many of the prophetic announcements are yet unfulfilled, but their absolute authenticity will be established when Christ returns in glory.

6. "To anoint the most Holy" definitely refers to the Holy of Holies in a reconstructed temple. The Jews will have a new temple which God will anoint and acknowledge at the beginning of the millennial age, as He did the tabernacle, and also the temple built by Solomon.

All of these things were promised by God through Daniel to Israel and are yet future, for he declared that they would follow the period of "seventy weeks."

There is universal agreement that the Hebrew word translated "weeks" in verse 24 actually means "sevens" and refers to sevens of years. Daniel's seventy weeks would then add up to 490 years. According to this it will be after a period of 490 years of God's special dealings with the Jewish people and the city of Jerusalem that the sixfold blessings enumerated in verse 24 will become a reality.

483 YEARS TO MESSIAH

Verse 25 goes on to tell us that from the date of the issuing of the decree to restore and rebuild Jerusalem until the appearance of the Messiah there would be a span of 69 sevens of years (seven weeks plus threescore and two equals 69). This amounts to 483 years, for 69 x 7 = 483. With that in mind, listen again to verse 25 of Daniel, chapter 9,

> Know, therefore, and understand, that from the going forth of the commandment to restore and to build Jerusalem unto the Messiah, the Prince, shall be seven weeks, and threescore and two weeks; the street shall be built again, and the wall, even in troublous times.

This has been literally fulfilled as history itself will testify.

Scholars are not completely agreed concerning which decree begins the time measurement here indicated. Some follow Sir Robert Anderson who calculated that from the time of the issuance of Artaxerxes' decree in 444 B.C. to the day of our Lord's triumphal entry into Jerusalem amounts to exactly 483 *prophetic* years. A "prophetic" year consists of 360 days and 483 such years would total 173,880 days. Others contend that we cannot be completely certain about some of these dates, and believe instead that the reckoning should begin with the return of Ezra to Jerusalem in 458 B.C. Using *standard chronological* years, 483 years from that point would bring us to the beginning of Christ's ministry at His baptism around A.D. 26. In either case we have a striking fulfillment of prophecy as the Messiah appeared on schedule. If we had all the facts and could construct a completely accurate chronology, we could pinpoint the exact date foreseen by the prophet Daniel, and the coming of the Lord would have perfectly coincided with it.

The Timeclock Stops

According to verse 26 there was to be an interruption in the "seventy weeks" of God's dealings with Israel. Daniel says,

> . . . after threescore and two weeks shall Messiah be cut off, but not for himself; and the people of the prince that shall come shall destroy the city and the sanctuary, and the end of

it shall be with a flood, and unto the end of the war
desolations are determined (Daniel 9:26).

This verse tells us about those things which will happen
after the 483 years, but *before* the beginning of the last
seven-year time division. It clearly portrays the crucifixion
of the Lord Jesus Christ and the subsequent destruction of
Jerusalem in A.D. 70. This prophecy declares that *after* the
69 sevens of years (483 years) Messiah was to be cut off,
and the city of Jerusalem destroyed. In other words, this
verse clearly places our Lord's crucifixion and the destruction of Jerusalem *after* the sixty-ninth "week," but *before*
the seventieth. This is history. Christ was crucified after
the 483 years, and Jerusalem was destroyed some 40 years
later, in A.D. 70. A "gap" then exists between the sixty-
ninth and seventieth "weeks." Some who do not accept the
premillennial view of the return of Christ have accused us
of importing this "gap" to bolster our position. However,
both the declaration of verse 26 and history itself make it
obvious that the seventieth week does not directly follow
the sixty-ninth. There was a "break" in God's dealings with
Israel. God's timeclock that had been ticking off the 69
weeks of Daniel's prophecy stopped, and will not commence
again until the Lord takes out the Church.

THE FUTURE 7 YEARS

Looking at verse 27 we see some very precise statements
concerning Israel's future during the seventieth week, when
God's plans and purposes for the nation will be renewed in
a very specific way. Daniel tells us that,

> . . . he [that is the false prince introduced in verse 26]
> shall confirm the covenant with many for one week; and in
> the midst of the week he shall cause the sacrifice and the

> oblation to cease, and for the overspreading of abominations
> he shall make it desolate, even until the consummation, and
> that determined shall be poured upon the desolate (Daniel
> 9:27).

The "he" in this verse refers back to the coming prince, the
one whose people (the Romans) destroyed Jerusalem and
the temple in A.D. 70. He will make a seven-year pact with
Israel. (Remember that these seventy "weeks" are related
to Daniel's people and his holy city.) The Jews, at least a
representative group, will be in the land of Palestine, and
they will feel secure in this agreement with the wicked
prince, who is the Antichrist. He will honor this contract for
about three and one-half years. During that time a temple
will be built by the Jews, and they will set up some form of
worship. Suddenly, however, this world dictator will turn
against them, and on the very wing of their temple he will
erect an image which he will insist they must worship.
Daniel predicted this when he said in verse 27,

> . . . in the midst of the week he shall cause the sacrifice and
> the oblation to cease, and for the overspreading of abomina-
> tions he shall make it desolate, even until the consummation,
> and that determined shall be poured upon the desolate (Dan-
> iel 9:27).

The final words found in this verse, "for the overspreading
of abominations he shall make it desolate," are clearly related to a prophecy the Lord Jesus Himself made concerning this abomination of desolation. We hear Him saying
in Matthew 24, verses 15 and 16,

> When ye, therefore, shall see the abomination of desolation,
> spoken of by Daniel the prophet, stand in the holy place
> (whosoever readeth, let him understand),
> Then let them who are in Judaea flee into the mountains.

Other Scripture passages, including II Thessalonians 2:4 and Revelation 13:14-18, indicate that an image will be erected by the coming Antichrist, and that refusal to worship this idol will trigger a period of dreadful persecution, primarily for the Jews, but for all the other inhabitants of the earth as well.

THE PROPHECY OF DANIEL 11

Before concluding this chapter, I would call your attention to the eleventh chapter of Daniel which tells us that Egypt and Syria are also involved in a very special way in God's prophetic program. In addition to a preview of Israel's history from the time of their subjugation by Persia onward, we see in Daniel 11 the rise of Alexander the Great, the division of his kingdom at his death, the appearance of Antiochus Epiphanes and his cruel persecution, and the Maccabean revolt. Many other historic details are foretold with astounding accuracy. All these things prophesied in the first 35 verses have been literally fulfilled.

Verses 36 through 45, however, point us to the future. Almost all Bible commentators, regardless of the position they take concerning the Antichrist and the return of Jesus Christ, agree that these predictions have never yet been fulfilled. I read, beginning at verse 40,

> And at the time of the end shall the king of the south push at him; and the king of the north shall come against him like a whirlwind, with chariots, and with horsemen, and with many ships; and he shall enter into the countries, and shall overflow and pass through.
>
> He shall enter also into the glorious land, and many countries shall be overthrown, but these shall escape out of his hand, even Edom, and Moab, and the chief of the children of Ammon.
>
> He shall stretch forth his hand also upon the countries, and the land of Egypt shall not escape.

> But he shall have power over the treasures of gold and of silver, and over all the precious things of Egypt; and the Libyans and the Ethiopians shall be at his steps.
>
> But tidings out of the east and out of the north shall trouble him; therefore, he shall go forth with great fury to destroy, and utterly to sweep away many.
>
> And he shall plant the tabernacles of his palace between the seas in the glorious holy mountain; yet he shall come to his end, and none shall help him (Daniel 11:40-45).

There are three powerful characters in this picture: the king of the south, the king of the north, and the king who is introduced in verse 36 as the one who "shall do according to his will," the Antichrist. "The king of the south" in the Bible is always Egypt, and "the king of the north" is Syria, probably in a confederacy with the other Arab nations. They will unite in their opposition to the Antichrist, but he will be victorious. Antichrist shall then pass through Palestine, permitting some countries to escape his vengeance, but plundering Egypt along with Libya and Ethiopia.

Now hear what Daniel says as he continues in verse 44 and predicts what is to follow,

> But tidings out of the east and out of the north shall trouble him; therefore, he shall go forth with great fury to destroy, and utterly to sweep away many.
>
> And he shall plant the tabernacles of his palace between the seas in the glorious holy mountain; yet he shall come to his end, and none shall help him (Daniel 11:44, 45).

While the Antichrist is engaged in securing his victory over the rebels in the Middle East, he will receive news from the east and the north which will trouble him. He will come up through Palestine with a fury and a rage that will lead him to destroy and exterminate many in the land. He shall build a palace on the Mount of Olives from which both the Mediterranean and the Dead Sea can be seen. This will be done in a blasphemous attempt to insult the true God, the very One to whom many of the Jews shall have turned. Here in the Holy Land, however, the Antichrist will meet with disaster. The Lord Himself shall bring about his overwhelming defeat.

Further details concerning the final doom of the Antichrist in Palestine are given in Zechariah 14. Jerome, writing in the 4th century, declared, "No one shall be able to assist the Antichrist as the Lord vents His fury upon him. . . . Antichrist is going to perish in that spot from which our Lord ascended to heaven."

Yes, the day is coming when Israel, Egypt and the Arab nations shall have a common enemy. This man, the Antichrist, shall cause them great suffering as he unwittingly becomes God's chastening rod. When God's purposes have been accomplished through him, however, the Lord will destroy him utterly.

What a comfort it is to know that although the world scene darkens and sin runs rampant on every hand, the day is coming when ". . . the earth shall be filled with the knowledge of the glory of the Lord, as the waters cover the sea" (Habakkuk 2:14).

The things which are transpiring before our eyes today should alert us to the lateness of the hour, the nearness of our Lord's return.

> And when these things begin to come to pass, then look up, and lift up your heads; for your redemption draweth near (Luke 21:28).

Chapter Seven

ISRAEL'S REPENTANCE AND RESTORATION

The descendants of Abraham were given the land of Canaan in a free, unconditional, and unchangeable grant from God. This can be very clearly seen in verses 7 and 8 of Genesis, chapter 17, where God declares,

> And I will establish my covenant between me and thee and thy seed after thee in their generations for an everlasting covenant, to be a God unto thee, and to thy seed after thee.
> And I will give unto thee, and to thy seed after thee, the land wherein thou art a sojourner, all the land of Canaan, for an everlasting possession; and I will be their God.

Not all of Abraham's offspring have a right to this promised land, however, since the Lord specifically identified the son through whom this promise would be realized. God said to Abraham in Genesis 21:12, ". . . in *Isaac* shall thy seed be called."

The rightful possessors of the land, then, are only those descendants of Abraham through Isaac, and these people are known to us today as Jews, or Israelites.

The unmistakable condition laid down by God Himself that, ". . . in Isaac shall thy seed be called," rules out the Arab nations as legitimate claimants to the land. Although the lineage of some of them can be traced to Abraham, it goes back not through Isaac, but rather through Ishmael. It was Ishmael, the son of Abraham by Hagar, who became the father of the Bedouins, the wandering nomadic tribes of the Middle East. Isaac, on the other hand, was the progenitor of the Jewish people also called Israelites. It was to them, through Abraham, Isaac and Jacob, that God gave the title deed to the land of Palestine.

The history of the Israelites is such that some dispute the identity of the Jews as the true Israel and relegate their promises and rights to others. You will recall that by a series of providential circumstances, including the sale of Joseph by his brethren into slavery, God arranged that the family of Jacob should spend 400 years in Egypt. Here they were able to live in isolation and become a great nation. When the time came for them to leave the land of Egypt, the Lord in His providence brought about conditions which made the people of Israel eager to leave. Through a series of supernatural judgments God secured their release and then miraculously guided them through forty years of wilderness wandering. He gave them His law, granted them entrance into Canaan, and helped them defeat their enemies.

However, Israel never fully obeyed God, and therefore did not enjoy the complete realization of His promises. Although He gave them a period of great blessing under the reign of David, and the power of the nation reached its zenith when Solomon was King, Solomon's luxurious living and expensive tastes placed a great burden of taxation upon the people. Under Rehoboam, Solomon's successor, the unrest led to a split into two separate kingdoms. The ten northern tribes who did not accept as king the descendants of David, soon fell into gross idolatry and vile pagan practices. The two southern tribes, Judah and Benjamin, retained the Davidic dynasty and the Divinely ordained temple worship, but also descended to forbidden forms of worship. Israel was conquered by Assyria in 721 B.C., and the most desirable people were taken captive into the various parts of the Assyrian empire. A similar fate befell Judah at the hands of Babylon in 586 B.C. some 140 years after Israel's captivity began.

Israel's Present State

Today some 2.7 million Jews are living in Palestine, and they to a great extent are reviving many of their distinctive historic features and customs. However, the religious faith of the vast majority is neither true Judaism nor Christianity. Only a few are orthodox Jews who seriously believe that the nation should live under the Mosaic Law in genuine expectation of the promised Messiah. Most of them hold to a modified and liberalized Judaism, and some are atheists. Very few accept Jesus Christ as the true Messiah or look for God literally to fulfill the Old Testament Scriptures sometime in the future. However, they still look upon the land of Palestine as the country of great promise for them.

The present condition of Israel was depicted by one of the prophets over twenty-five hundred years ago. Hosea's wife, Gomer, had been unfaithful to him. She left him and had lived wickedly, falling so low that she was now offered for sale at a slave market. Hosea purchased her and brought her back to his home. He told her that she would no longer be able to consort with her former lovers, and that she would abide in his home for many days, but not as his wife. She would be free from her former sinful companions, but would not be in true marital union with Hosea. By application of this principle to Israel, he said,

> For the children of Israel shall abide many days without a king, and without a prince, and without a sacrifice, and without an image, and without an ephod, and without teraphim (Hosea 3:4).

From the year A.D. 70 onward this has been true. The Jewish people have been without a king or a prince. They have had no united sacrificial system, but they have also been free from the superstitious relics of heathenism as represented by the image, ephod, and teraphim. They have not continued in their own ancient faith, but neither have they embraced the false religious systems of others.

JUDGMENT PROPHESIED BY MOSES

The book of Deuteronomy is both a moving personal document and a striking prophecy. Moses, knowing that he would soon die, reiterated God's covenant with Israel and also faced the new generation which was to enter Canaan with the demand that they pledge their loyalty to Joshua, his divinely appointed successor. He pronounced glorious blessings upon them for obedience, and dire curses for disobedience. In addition to this, he gave a detailed picture of Israel's future which is amazing in its accuracy.

Moses predicted that the Israelites would not obey God, and that they would be removed from their land, scattered among the nations and delivered to their enemies who would bitterly persecute them. Listen to Moses as he declares in Deuteronomy 28:63-67,

> And it shall come to pass, that as the Lord rejoiced over you to do you good, and to multiply you, so the Lord will rejoice over you to destroy you, and to bring you to nothing; and ye shall be plucked from off the land to which thou goest to possess it.
>
> And the Lord shall scatter thee among all people, from the one end of the earth even unto the other. . . .
>
> And among these nations shalt thou find no ease, neither shall the sole of thy foot have rest; but the Lord shall give thee there a trembling heart, and failing of eyes, and sorrow of mind.

And thy life shall hang in doubt before thee; and thou shalt fear day and night, and shalt have no assurance of thy life:
In the morning thou shalt say, Would God it were evening! and at evening thou shalt say, Would God it were morning!

This is indeed one of the most amazing prophecies in the entire Word of God, and all of it has been accomplished to the letter.

RESTORATION PREDICTED

That day when the nation of Israel would return to the land of Canaan was also foretold by Moses. He said:

And it shall come to pass, when all these things are come upon thee, the blessing and the curse, which I have set before thee, and thou shalt call them to mind among all the nations, to which the Lord thy God hath driven thee,
And shalt return unto the Lord thy God. . . .
That then the Lord thy God will turn thy captivity, and have compassion upon thee, and will return and gather thee from all the nations where the Lord thy God hath scattered thee.
And the Lord thy God will circumcise thine heart, and the heart of thy seed, to love the Lord thy God with all thine heart, and with all thy soul, that thou mayest live (Deuteronomy 30:1-3, 6).

Comparing this prediction with that of Ezekiel 36:24-28, and the prophet's vision of the dry bones in chapter 37, it appears that although a remnant will return to the land in unbelief, the complete regathering of the Israelites and their permanent establishment in the land will not be realized until they have genuinely repented and returned to God.

Down through the centuries the Jewish people in general have ignored some of their own Scriptures. Speaking of the Messiah, Psalm 22 declared, ". . . they pierced my hands and my feet" (Psalm 22:16).

Concerning the coming of Christ, Isaiah wrote: "But he was wounded for our transgressions, he was bruised for our iniquities; the chastisement for our peace was upon him, and with his stripes we are healed" (Isaiah 53:5).

REPENTANCE BEFORE RESTORATION

Zechariah 12:10 tells us that someday the remnant of Israel which has survived the tribulation will see the Savior, recognize Him, and weep tears of repentance and gratitude. Here are the prophet's own words,

> And I will pour upon the house of David, and upon the inhabitants of Jerusalem, the Spirit of grace and of supplications; and they shall look upon me whom they have pierced, and they shall mourn for him, as one mourneth for his only son, and shall be in bitterness for him, as one that is in bitterness for his firstborn (Zechariah 12:10).

At first sight, Old Testament passages such as this would seem to indicate that the return of the Messiah *causes* Israel to repent. Other verses make clear, however, that it is through the fires of affliction that the remnant turns to God, and Peter plainly told the Jews that the promised times of refreshing, the millennial age, will not come until they turn to Christ. We hear Peter preaching in Acts 3, beginning at verse 19,

> Repent, therefore, and be converted, that your sins may be blotted out, when the times of refreshing shall come from the presence of the Lord;
> And he shall send Jesus Christ, who before was preached unto you (Acts 3:19, 20).

The New Scofield Reference Bible in the margin gives us the proper translation of these words. It renders verses 19 and 20 in this way, "Repent . . . *so that* the times of refreshing shall come from the presence of the Lord, and he shall send . . . Jesus Christ." This is unquestionably the proper translation of the Greek text. We must therefore interpret the statements of the Old Testament in the light of his clear declaration. Israel's conversion will precede the glorious return of Christ.

The great tribulation, which will follow the rapture of the Church, will be the means of Israel's conversion and this will precede the glorious second coming of the Lord Jesus Christ to this earth. During the tribulation, the world will experience its most grievous time in history. The opening of the fourth seal (Revelation 6:7, 8) brings out the death of one-fourth of mankind. On the basis of our present population this means that some 750 million people will die through various judgments. The judgment of the sixth trumpet (Revelation 9:13-21) destroys one-third of those who survive the earlier plagues. Zechariah 13, verse 9, tells us that only one-third of the Jews will survive this period of great tribulation.

The brighter side of the picture can be seen in chapter 7 of Revelation. God seals 144,000 Jews who apparently turn to Him in genuine faith early in the tribulation, and they become His witnesses. God supernaturally protects them, and they boldly proclaim His message. As a result of their ministry, a great multitude from every nation, kindred and tongue are saved (Revelation 7:9), many of whom will die in that day of trouble (Revelation 7:14). God, however, will preserve a remnant of saved Jews who will enter the millennium. The 144,000 who are sealed in Revelation 7 are still intact when we see them in Revelation 14. This is the nucleus of a godly remnant who will welcome our Lord when He comes to reign.

Unbelievers Purged

Those Israelites who survive the great tribulation without turning to Christ, who have worshiped the Antichrist and his image (Revelation 13:8), will be purged out and shall not enter the kingdom age. Ezekiel 20:34 and 38 declare.

> And I will bring you out from the peoples, and will gather you out of the countries in which ye are scattered, with a mighty hand, and with an outstretched arm, and with fury poured out.
>
> And I will purge out from among you the rebels, and them that transgress against me; I will bring them forth out of the country where they sojourn, and they shall not enter into the land of Israel; and ye shall know that I am the Lord.

Thus only a relatively small percentage of the Israelites who go into the tribulation will live through it to enter the millennium. Only those who have been truly born again through faith in Christ shall enter that glorious kingdom age.

The government which the Lord Jesus will establish upon the earth will have its center in Jerusalem. Isaiah prophesied of that day with these words,

> . . . for out of Zion shall go forth the law, and the word of the Lord from Jerusalem.
>
> And he shall judge among the nations, and shall rebuke many peoples; and they shall beat their swords into plowshares, and their spears into pruning hooks; nation shall not lift up sword against nation, neither shall they learn war any more (Isaiah 2:3, 4).

Canaan Restored and Transformed

Moreover, restored Israel shall inherit the land God gave to Abraham and his seed for an everlasting possession. Ezekiel declared,

> Thus saith the Lord God: In the day that I shall have cleansed you from all your iniquities, I will also cause you to dwell in the cities, and the wastes shall be built.
>
> Then the nations that are left round about you shall know that I, the Lord, build the ruined places, and plant that which was desolate. I, the Lord, have spoken it, and I will do it (Ezekiel 36:33, 36).

In Zechariah 14 we have a very graphic description of the tremendous topographical changes which will take place in the land of Palestine when the Lord descends to the Mount of Olives. The prophet pictures the armies of the nations converging upon Jerusalem for battle. Just when all appears very dark for the city of Jerusalem, the Lord Jesus returns, His feet standing upon the Mount of Olives. The armies of the enemy nations are destroyed as described in verses 12 through 15. A great earthquake brings about a radical transformation of the entire land. The mountains that now surround Jerusalem will be flattened into a plain, and Jerusalem will be elevated above the rest of the terrain. The city which is now nestled between the mountains will be situated on a high hill, and from it will flow living water into both the Dead Sea and the Mediterranean. This supernatural water supply will break forth from the ground in Jerusalem, and become a great stream. Zechariah predicted that,

> . . . his feet [the feet of the Lord Jesus] shall stand in that day upon the Mount of Olives, which is before Jerusalem on the east, and the Mount of Olives shall cleave in its midst toward the east and toward the west. . . .
>
> And it shall be, in that day, that living waters shall go out from Jerusalem; half of them toward the former sea, and half of them toward the hinder sea; in summer and in winter shall it be.
>
> All the land shall be turned like the Arabah from Geba to

Rimmon south of Jerusalem; and it shall be lifted up, and inhabited in its place. . . .

And men shall dwell in it, and there shall be no more utter destruction; but Jerusalem shall be safely inhabited (Zechariah 14:4, 8, 10, 11).

BLESSING FOR THE NATIONS

Even Egypt and Assyria, bitter enemies of Israel down through the ages, will have a part in the blessings of this glorious age. Isaiah 19:22-25 contains a wonderful message of hope for all the peoples of the Middle East. Listen to this prophecy:

And the Lord shall smite Egypt; he shall smite and heal it: and they shall return even to the Lord, and he shall be entreated by them, and shall heal them.

In that day shall Israel be the third with Egypt and with Assyria, even a blessing in the midst of the land,

Whom the Lord of hosts shall bless, saying, Blessed be Egypt, my people, and Assyria, the work of my hands, and Israel, mine inheritance.

The Bible expressly declares that Egypt shall someday turn to God, and along with Assyria and Israel enjoy great prosperity in the millennial kingdom. Inasmuch as Assyria does not exist by that name today, many commentators agree that it has reference to Syria and her neighboring powers. Though Israel is mentioned as "the third," in verse 24, this does not mean the third in power or rank. The priority of Israel is still indicated in that Israel is called God's "inheritance." Peace will come to the troubled Middle East. The Arab nations, and Israel and Egypt shall live together in beautiful harmony. God will call Egypt "his people," and the land will know blessedness beyond anything it has yet experienced.

That which God has in mind for Egypt and Assyria will

be shared by all other nations. All the earth shall participate in the benefits of the reign of Jesus Christ. Looking forward to this day of universal blessing, the Psalmist said:

> Say among the nations that the Lord reigneth. The world also shall be established that it shall not be moved; he shall judge the peoples righteously.
>
> Let the heavens rejoice, and let the earth be glad; let the sea roar, and the fullness thereof.
>
> Let the field be joyful, and all that is therein; then shall all the trees of the forest rejoice
>
> Before the Lord; for he cometh, for he cometh to judge the earth; he shall judge the world with righteousness, and the peoples with his truth (Psalm 96:10-13).

These wonderful prophetic truths are thrilling to those who know Jesus Christ, but are without blessing to you if you are unsaved. The frightening prospect of a dreadful tribulation period and an eternal Hell looms before you. To you we extend an invitation to receive Jesus Christ as your Savior. He died for you, and if you believe on Him God will forgive your sin, adopt you into His family, and give you eternal life.

Why not bow your head in prayer and settle this matter of your soul's salvation? Here is a suggested word of prayer which you might offer: "Lord Jesus, I know that I am a sinner and could never save myself. I believe that Thou didst die for me and shed Thy blood for my sin, and that Thou didst rise again from the dead. And now I am receiving Thee as my Savior, my Lord, my only hope of salvation. Lord, be merciful to me a sinner, and save me according to the promise of Thy Word. Amen."

If you prayed this and really meant it, you are saved. The Bible says, "For whosoever shall call upon the name of the Lord shall be saved" (Romans 10:13).

Chapter Eight

THREE DECISIVE WARS

The Bible tells us about three great end-time battles. The first one is depicted in Ezekiel 38 and 39. It is an invasion of Palestine by a coalition of nations from the far north. The second battle predicted in connection with the coming of Christ is one in which "all nations" gather specifically against Jerusalem. It is described in a number of Old Testament passages and in the book of the Revelation. This is the Battle of Armageddon. The third and last conflict of Biblical prophecy is depicted in Revelation 20:7-10. It will take place after the millennial reign of Jesus Christ comes to a close and just before the eternal order is established. Our understanding of the prophetic Scriptures will be greatly enhanced by a clear picture of these three battles as they relate to one another.

Invasion From the North

The first of these battles is described vividly by Ezekiel, and by Ezekiel alone. In the 38th and 39th chapters of his prophetic book, many details are given which we cannot completely explain at the present time. This is not strange because we find that very often prophecy is so presented that the general picture is clear, but many of the fine points cannot be fitted in until the actual fulfillment comes. Ezekiel says:

> Therefore, son of man, prophesy and say unto Gog, Thus saith the Lord God: In that day when my people of Israel dwell safely, shalt thou not know it?
>
> And thou shalt come from thy place out of the north parts, thou, and many peoples with thee, all of them riding upon horses, a great company, and a mighty army;
>
> And thou shalt come up against my people of Israel, like a cloud to cover the land; it shall be in the latter days, and I will bring thee against my land, that the nations may know me, when I shall be sanctified in thee, O Gog, before their eyes.
>
> And I will enter into judgment against him with pestilence and with blood; and I will rain upon him, and upon his hordes, and upon the many peoples that are with him, an over-flowing rain, and great hailstones, fire and brimstone.
>
> Thus will I magnify myself, and sanctify myself; and I will be known in the eyes of many nations, and they shall know that I am the Lord (Ezekiel 38:14-16; 22, 23).

We can confidently make four brief affirmations on the basis of these words.

1. This invasion of Palestine will occur in the "latter days" (verses 8, 16), and when Israel is dwelling in safety, feeling secure (verses 10, 11, 14).

2. This invasion comes from the "north parts"; that is, the area farthest north in relation to Palestine. A glance at your map will immediately show you that Russia is the nation which meets this qualification.

3. Many other nations will join with Russia in this effort: ". . . many peoples with thee. . ." (verse 15).

4. God will be glorified before the world of mankind as He brings about the supernatural and overwhelming defeat of the invaders (verses 16, 22, 23).

In the Latter Days

We know that this prophecy has not yet been fulfilled. Nothing like this has taken place, and the time for its fulfillment is designated as "in the latter days." The "latter days" of Israel's history will not arrive until the Church is raptured, and God once again takes up His dealing with this nation. Moreover, the conditions at present do not meet the requirements of this prophecy, for Israel is not "dwelling in peace and safety." It is maintaining a standing army, and must be ever ready to ward off an invasion by Arab or Egyptian forces. The situation in the Middle East must change radically from what it is today before the prophecy of Ezekiel 38 and 39 can be fulfilled.

A False Assurance of Peace

In order to determine the time these northern powers will invade Palestine, we must study the prophetic Scriptures to see when the Jewish people living in Palestine will no longer feel the need to be on guard for fear of hostile neighbors. This situation will prevail only when present enemies become friendly, or when some great world power, feared by all the nations, gives Israel absolute assurance of protection. Daniel clearly teaches us that the second of these alternatives will take place. In his well-known prophecy of the "seventy weeks" which are determined upon the Jewish people and their holy city, he tells us that after the Messiah has been "cut off" (by crucifixion) ". . . the people of the prince that shall come shall destroy the city and the sanctuary. . . ." These words definitely predicted that Jerusalem and the temple would be destroyed, and they were literally fulfilled by the Romans in A.D. 70.

However, you will notice that the prophet makes it clear

that this "prince who shall come" was not Titus, the man who led the Romans in A.D. 70. Often in the prophetic Scriptures we find a double reference. The prophet saw two future events, the first one a shadow of the greater and final fulfillment of the prophecy. "The *people* of the prince," (that is, the Romans) did destroy the city and temple. The prince in view, however, did not appear on the scene when the Jews were slaughtered and scattered by the Roman armies. This "prince that shall come" is the man who will be the end-time world ruler, the head of the Federation of Western Nations which will constitute the revived Roman Empire. You will recall from a previous study of Daniel 9 that God's timeclock for Israel stopped when the Jews rejected Jesus Christ. Thus the "seventieth week" is to be fulfilled at some future time. Looking forward to the activity of this Roman prince in the latter days of Israel's history, Daniel says,

> And he [Antichrist] shall confirm the covenant with many [the Jews] for one week [seven years]; and in the midst of the week he shall cause the sacrifice and the oblation to cease, and for the overspreading of abominations he shall make it desolate, even until the consummation, and that determined shall be poured upon the desolate (Daniel 9:27).

The seven-year tribulation period is thus clearly divided into two segments of three and one-half years each. For about three and one-half years the world ruler will pose as the best friend the Jewish people have ever had. However, he will suddenly turn against them and inaugurate a period of bitter persecution which Jeremiah calls "the time of Jacob's trouble" (Jeremiah 30:7). Israel certainly will not be dwelling in peace and safety once this "beast" of the prophetic Scriptures turns against them. However, the first half of this seven-year period will meet the requirements of

Ezekiel's prophecy, for Israel will then be living with a false feeling of peace and security. Therefore, we conclude that this invasion from the far north will occur at some time *after* the Church is raptured, but *before* Antichrist turns against the people of Israel.

INVADERS DESTROYED

These northern armies will be supernaturally and completely destroyed by God before they reach Jerusalem. This astounding destruction of Russia as a military power will make a tremendous impact upon Israel and the nations. In Ezekiel 39:21, 22 we read:

> And I will set my glory among the nations, and all the nations shall see my judgment that I have executed, and my hand that I have laid upon them.
> So the house of Israel shall know that I am the Lord, their God, from that day and forward.

PRELUDE TO ARMAGEDDON

Undoubtedly the military defeat of Russia will be a factor in bringing about a great turning to God on the part of both Jews and Gentiles. The evil political genius who will have gained world power will naturally be infuriated when he sees people turning to God. Revelation 13 portrays him as the devil's man who will desire that men worship him as God. When Russia is out of the way as a world power he will dare demand the worship of mankind, and will bitterly persecute those who refuse. He will inaugurate a program of persecution so widespread and thorough that according to Zechariah 13, verse 9, only one-third of the Jews will survive this brief three-and-one-half-year period.

Moreover, Revelation 7 pictures a great unnumbered multitude of Gentiles who will turn to Christ, and who will die for their faith during this dreadful time. However, though Russia will have been defeated, and Antichrist will be able to exercise absolute and ruthless power, all will not continue to go well with him and his henchmen. As the brief three and one-half years of his absolute authority draws to its close, the bowls of God's fierce wrath described in Revelation 16 will fall upon his kingdom. Life will become exceedingly difficult, and the nations will begin to seethe under the strain.

Daniel 11 gives us a picture of Antichrist when he comes to his place of absolute power, and of rebellion he will encounter in the Middle East as nations to the north and south of Palestine attack his armies stationed there.

> And the king shall do according to his will; and he shall exalt himself, and magnify himself above every god, and shall speak marvelous things against the God of gods, and shall prosper till the indignation be accomplished; for that which is determined shall be done.
>
> Neither shall he regard the gods of his father, nor the desire of women, nor regard any gods; for he shall magnify himself above all.
>
> But in his estate shall he honor the god of fortresses; and a god whom his fathers knew not shall he honor with gold, and silver, and with precious stones, and pleasant things.
>
> Thus shall he do in the strongest fortresses with a foreign god, whom he shall acknowledge and increase with glory; and he shall cause them to rule over many, and shall divide the land for gain (Daniel 11:36-39).

In this passage we see the Antichrist magnifying himself above the true God and all the gods men have historically worshiped, having no regard for established religions, and promoting the worship of himself. Strangely enough he will also honor a "god of fortresses" and engage in religious practices of a superstitious nature. (We will omit a detailed discussion of some aspects of these verses lest we lose ourselves in fine points that are admittedly obscure at the present time.) Inasmuch as this portrait is similar to that which we find in Revelation 13 where we are specifically told that he will continue "forty and two months" (Revelation 13:5), we have good reason to apply the prophecies of Daniel 11 verses 36 through 45 to the last part of the tribulation period, the close of his regime.

The rebellions which form a portion of the series of events which culminate at Armageddon are described in Daniel 11 verses 40 through 45:

> And at the time of the end shall the king of the south push at him [the willful king introduced in verse 36]; and the king of the north shall come against him like a whirlwind, with chariots, and with horsemen, and with many ships; and he [the willful king] shall enter into the countries, and shall overflow and pass through.
>
> He [Antichrist, the willful king] shall enter also into the glorious land, and many countries shall be overthrown, but these shall escape out of his hand, even Edom, and Moab, and the chief of the children of Ammon.
>
> He shall stretch forth his hand also upon the countries, and the land of Egypt shall not escape.
>
> But he shall have power over the treasures of gold and of silver, and over all the precious things of Egypt; and the Libyans and the Ethiopians shall be at his steps.
>
> But tidings out of the east and out of the north shall trouble him; therefore, he shall go forth with great fury to destroy, and utterly to sweep away many.
>
> And he shall plant the tabernacles of his palace between the seas in the glorious holy mountain; yet he shall come to his end, and none shall help him.

He apparently will be successful in defeating all his rebellious enemies, and will pitch his royal tent on the slopes of the Mount of Olives in an act of defiance against God. Flushed with these victories he will boldly seek to destroy the 144,000 sealed witnesses whom God has miraculously preserved. In Revelation 14 we see them on Mt. Zion, safe and unharmed. Therefore, the armies of men from all nations who hate God will assemble near Jerusalem in the valley of Megiddo to make their attack. Blinded by sin and deceived by demons, they join Antichrist in this their final act of rebellion against God. Revelation 16 describes this event.

> And I saw three unclean spirits, like frogs, come out of the mouth of the dragon, and out of the mouth of the beast, and out of the mouth of the false prophet.
>
> For they are the spirits of demons, working miracles, that go forth unto the kings of the earth and of the whole world, to gather them to the battle of that great day of God Almighty.
>
> And he gathered them together into a place called in the Hebrew tongue Armageddon (Revelation 16:13, 14, 16).

CHRIST'S VICTORY AT ARMAGEDDON

This is the Battle of Armageddon. It will mark the close of the Great Tribulation, bring about the complete defeat of Antichrist's armies, and seal the personal doom of the Beast (Antichrist) and the False Prophet.

Listen to Zechariah's graphic description of the destruction of the assembled armies:

> Behold, the day of the Lord cometh, and thy spoil shall be divided in the midst of thee.
>
> For I will gather all nations against Jerusalem to battle; and the city shall be taken, and the houses rifled, and the women ravished; and half of the city shall go forth into captivity, and the residue of the people shall not be cut off from the city.
>
> Then shall the Lord go forth, and fight against those nations, as when he fought in the day of battle.
>
> And his feet shall stand in that day upon the Mount of Olives, which is before Jerusalem on the east, and the Mount of Olives shall cleave in its midst toward the east and toward the west, and there shall be a very great valley; and half of the mountain shall remove toward the north, and half of it toward the south.

> And the Lord shall be king over all the earth; in that day shall there be one Lord, and his name one (Zechariah 14:1-4, 9).

John tells us of the doom of the Beast and False Prophet in these words,

> And the beast was taken, and with him the false prophet that wrought miracles before him, with which he deceived them that had received the mark of the beast, and them that worshiped his image. These both were cast alive into a lake of fire burning with brimstone (Revelation 19:20).

THE FINAL REBELLION

Coming now to the third great end-time battle, we find that this last battle of all mankind's history occurs after the millennium, and is described in Revelation 20:7-10,

> And when the thousand years are ended, Satan shall be loosed out of his prison,
>
> And shall go out to deceive the nations which are in the four quarters of the earth, Gog and Magog, to gather them together to battle; the number of whom is as the sand of the sea.
>
> And they went up on the breadth of the earth, and compassed the camp of the saints about, and the beloved city; and fire came down from God out of heaven, and devoured them.
>
> And the devil that deceived them was cast into the lake of fire and brimstone, where the beast and the false prophet are, and shall be tormented day and night forever and ever.

GOG AND MAGOG

The fact that the names "Gog and Magog" appear in this passage does not indicate that this is the same battle described in Ezekiel 38, 39. In Ezekiel the time is in the latter years *before* the kingdom is established over the earth, while this battle of Revelation 20:7-10 occurs *after* the millennial age. Moreover, the invading armies described in Ezekiel come only from the "north parts," while in Revelation they come from the "four quarters" of the earth. Because of this we must reassert that though the names "Gog and Magog" appear in both of these Scriptures, the actual wars described are separated by a period of more than one thousand years.

After the one thousand years has ended, Satan will be released from the bottomless pit for a short time. He will find multitudes who were born during the millennium, and who obeyed the Lord only because of compulsion. They will be eager to rebel against this One who will have so effectively enforced right conduct. They will be deceived by Satan into thinking that perhaps they can overcome Christ and His people. John uses the words "Gog and Magog" to indicate that the rebelling forces will include both political leaders and the people. Gog refers to princes, or leaders, while Magog represents the people. Apparently some who will have rendered outward obedience in positions of influence during the millennium will welcome the opportunity to revolt against Christ. They will attack the saints and the holy city, but will meet sudden and supernatural destruction. Satan will be cast into the lake of fire from which there will be no reprieve, and from which he will never be released.

No Spiritual Transformation by Punishment

This last insurrection will demonstrate that no moral agent who hardens himself against God can be reformed by punishment. Remember that during the millennial age Satan will be in the bottomless pit, yet he will emerge from it with the same wicked character as before. He will again deceive men, cause rebellion, and seek to dethrone God that he may bring in universal anarchy.

Man's Utter Depravity

This final revolt also teaches us that the Old Adamic nature is hopelessly depraved and corrupt. After man sinned while being tested under conscience, corruption and violence filled the earth until God had to send a flood. When God tested men under the restraining influence of government, they went into idolatry, turning their backs upon their Creator. When God gave mankind the Law to show him his utter depravity, men made it a system of works to earn salvation, and finally, casting off all restraint, they crucified the Lord of glory.

Today, under grace, man does not appreciate God's mercy, rejects the Gospel, and goes ever deeper into his sin. Finally, even in the millennial age, under the righteous rule of Jesus Christ, those who are not saved will chafe under His divine government. They will willingly join Satan in this last act of rebellion. All of this emphasizes the fact that the heart of man is incurably evil. It demonstrates indeed that "the carnal mind is not subject to the law of God, neither indeed can be," and that all men need to be born again through the Word and the Spirit of God.

Chapter Nine

RUSSIA'S CRUSHING DEFEAT

The globe upon which we live is constantly becoming smaller. No, it is not actually shrinking in circumference, but the old geographical barriers which once separated continents and nations do not mean much any more. It takes only minutes to traverse oceans, deserts, and mountains. Intercontinental ballistic missiles make every nation on earth vulnerable to an enemy nuclear attack at any moment. World leaders are under constant tension as wars break out everywhere. Thinking men wonder how long these battles will continue before they lead to the horror of another World War which they fear could annihilate mankind.

In addition to the tensions due to the international situation we have a terrifying increase in crime, a collapse in morals, and a general spirit of lawlessness. All of this has resulted in multiplied nervous breakdowns, mental disorders, and suicides. Many men who were optimistic about mankind's future twenty years ago, now are displaying their feelings of utter despair. However, the vast majority of mankind go blithely on their way in self-indulgence, closing their eyes to the real situation.

A Solemn and Honest Approach

Instructed Bible-believing Christians are the only people who can be realistic and yet optimistic. We do not close our eyes to the facts as they are. We know that the situation is precisely what the Bible predicted it would be, and we believe that the prophetic Scriptures tell us some very specific things about the future for us as individuals and for the nations.

In this chapter we will consider what God's Word declares about the coming defeat of Russia and her allies. As I approach the subject I know that some of you are a bit skeptical whenever a Bible teacher begins discussing prophecies of present happenings. You have perhaps heard men twist Bible passages to fit into the current picture. You may also remember predictions, made in a bold and authoritative manner, and you can point out to me that they never materialized. We can understand your attitude, and are very well aware of the fact that some who profess to be men of God have been guilty of these practices. In some cases, it has been due to ignorance on their part. However, sometimes unscrupulous men who do not really know God have deceitfully used the Word of God to gain a following. I want to assure you that what we preach about prophetic themes is the result of careful study, and that we are seeking to be completely honest before God. We tremble at the thought of a careless and deceitful use of God's holy Word.

Russia Identified

It is with reverence then that we turn to Ezekiel 38 and 39, which describe the overwhelming and supernatural destruction of the armies that come from the far north to attack Palestine. We believe that we have good reason to identify these armies as belonging to Russia and some allied nations. In Ezekiel 38:2-6 we read,

> Son of man, set thy face against Gog, of the land of Magog, the chief prince of Meshech and Tubal, and prophesy against him,
>
> And say, Thus saith the Lord God: Behold, I am against thee, O Gog, the chief prince of Meshech and Tubal,
>
> And I will turn thee back, and put hooks into thy jaws, and I will bring thee forth, and all thine army, horses, and horsemen, all of them clothed with all sorts of armor, even a great company with bucklers and shields, all of them handling swords:
>
> Persia, Cush, and Put with them; all of them with shield and helmet;
>
> Gomer, and all its hordes; the house of Togarmah of the north quarters, and all its hordes; and many peoples with thee.

Verses 2 and 3 contain some proper nouns which we believe establish the identity of the leading nation in this attack as modern Russia. We will examine each of these proper nouns, and will ask that you consider them carefully with us in order that you may determine whether or not our conclusion is correct.

1. "Gog" is the symbolic name of the man who heads this northern confederacy of nations. By itself it tells us nothing about the identity of the nations involved.

2. "Magog" is the symbolic name of his people, the land over which he rules. There is almost universal agreement that Magog refers to the land area north of the Caucasus Mountains. *The New Schaff Herzog Encyclopedia of Religious Knowledge* says, "A stricter geographical location would place Magog's dwelling between Armenia and Media, perhaps on the shores of Araxes. But the people seem to have extended farther north across the Caucasus, filling there the extreme northern horizon of the Hebrews" (Ezekiel

38:15; 39:2). A look at any world map will clearly identify this area as present-day Russia.

3. *"Rosh"* is not found in our King James Version, because the King James translators took this word as an adjective meaning "chief." Many of the finest grammarians, however, insist that here it is a proper noun, and therefore should read, ". . . Gog . . . prince of Rosh, Meshech and Tubal. . ." (Ezekiel 38:3). Gesenius, a world-renowned authority on the Hebrew language, in his widely used lexicon states, "Rosh — proper name of a northern nation, mentioned with Tubal and Meshech, undoubtedly the Russians, who are mentioned by Byzantine writers of the tenth century, under the name of 'the Rhos' (in Greek), dwelling to the north of Taurus." He goes on to point out that Arabic writers also make this same identification. Many other notable authorities confirm this conclusion of Gesenius.

4. "Meshech" appears in the Bible first as one of the sons of Japheth (Genesis 10:2). It is an ancient tribal name for Moscow. Many philologists feel it is related to the Moschi, a people who inhabited part of the country between the Black and Caspian Seas. From this word "Moschi" came a later designation of these people as Muscovites, and from this the name Moscow.

5. "Tubal" is often regarded as an ancient tribal name from which the former eastern capital of Russia, Tobolsk, is derived. Tobolsk was one of Russia's most famous cities. Gesenius, whose Hebrew lexicon is still regarded as one of the very best in existence, contends that Meshech and Tubal are related to present-day Moscow and Tobolsk.

The Clinching Consideration

These conclusions concerning the derivation of our present-day names — Russia, Moscow, and Tobolsk — are not unanimously accepted by scholars. In fact, some go so far as to call this "philological nonsense." The fact remains, however, that no evidence can be brought to bear to show that Gesenius and others like him were in error, and many of the finest linguists concur with those who insist that there is a relationship between these ancient tribal names and present-day Russia. However, even if one does not accept these linguistic conclusions, the identification of Russia is clear on the basis of the well nigh universal acceptance of Magog as the symbolic name of the land north of the Caucasus, and by the geographical location as given by Ezekiel: "The uttermost parts of the north" (Ezekiel 38:6, 15; 39:2 — marginal rendering in *The New Scofield Reference Bible*). My father a few years ago stated this in his usual clear and concise manner:

"In all these passages, Gog is said to be north of Palestine. Right here we would remind you that directions in the Bible are *always* given in relation to Palestine. Palestine is the geographic center of the earth's surface, and all directions start in this land, so that south in the Bible *always* means south of Palestine, north is always north of Palestine, and so with east and west. In the Bible, Gog and the land of Magog are located as *north* of Palestine, and can refer to nothing else than Russia and her allies. If you will draw a straight line from Jerusalem to the North Pole on your world map or globe, this line will pass right through the city of Moscow.

"Both Moscow and Jerusalem are located in the same meridian, just a few seconds west of the fortieth meridian. The northern armies, who will meet their waterloo when they invade Palestine in the latter days, can be none else than the communistic block under the leadership of Russia."

Russian Allies

We need not spend a great deal of time specifying the names of the nations which will join Russia in its march down into Palestine. Persia is present-day Iran. Cush and Put cannot be identified with absolute certainty, but most likely are nations that will be adjacent to Iran. Gomer is almost universally among Jewish historians looked upon as present-day Germany, at least the eastern part. Togarmah is usually identified as Turkey. These nations and many others with them will join Russia as the great move to conquer Palestine takes place.

Miraculous Intervention

The devastating defeat of these northern armies will be accomplished by God Himself. Ezekiel describes the manner in which God will pour out His wrath upon these invading forces.

> For in my jealousy and in the fire of my wrath have I spoken, Surely in that day there shall be a great shaking in the land of Israel,
>
> So that the fish of the sea, and the fowls of the heavens, and the beasts of the field, and all creeping things that creep upon the earth, and all the men that are upon the face of the earth, shall shake at my presence, and the mountains shall be thrown down, and the steep places shall fall, and every wall shall fall to the ground.
>
> And I will call for a sword against him throughout all my mountains, saith the Lord God; every man's sword shall be against his brother.
>
> And I will enter into judgment against him with pestilence and with blood; and I will rain upon him, and upon his hordes, and upon the many peoples that are with him, an overflowing rain, and great hailstones, fire, and brimstone (Ezekiel 38:19-22).

The earth around Palestine will tremble severely. This will throw the soldiers into such a panic that they will insanely kill one another. In addition to this, sudden diseases will strike them, rain and hail will come down upon them violently, and fire and brimstone shall erupt in their midst. Therefore, these armies will be destroyed without even being attacked by enemy nations.

A GREAT TURNING TO GOD

Think of the impact this will make upon the people of the world when the news reaches them. Thousands among the nations will acknowledge that the God of the Bible, the One whom the atheistic Communists have denied, is indeed the Living God. Jehovah through Ezekiel declares,

> Thus will I magnify myself, and sanctify myself; and I will be known in the eyes of many nations, and they shall know that I am the Lord (Ezekiel 38:23).

Among the Jews this will be a sign from God to lead vast numbers of them to faith in Jesus Christ. They will realize that the prophetic Scriptures are being fulfilled, and through the ministry of the 144,000 sealed Jews of Revelation 7, and of the two witnesses of Revelation 11, the majority of them will turn back to the God of their fathers. Ezekiel 39:7 declares,

> So will I make my holy name known in the midst of my people, Israel, and I will not let them pollute my holy name any more; and the nations shall know that I am the Lord, the Holy One in Israel.

GRAVE BUT ENCOURAGING PROSPECT

Friends, we are fast approaching that time which the prophets called the "Day of the Lord." One of these days

God is going to step down into history and intervene in an open and wondrous manner. For centuries men have sought to solve world problems, but have utterly failed. No person should be unwilling to acknowledge the desperate wickedness and woeful inadequacy of fallen mankind. God has given man ample time to demonstrate this, and if God did not intervene, man would ultimately annihilate himself. However, God will inaugurate a brief program in which He will take things out of the hands of men, and by which He will usher in the glorious one thousand year period we call the millennium.

The next event in God's plan is the rapture of the Church. The prophetic Scriptures give us many details concerning that which follows. They inform us that the time is coming when the world of mankind will worship a man who claims to be God and exercises universal political power. Revelation 13:4 tells us,

> And they worshiped the dragon who gave power unto the beast; and they worshiped the beast, saying, Who is like the beast? Who is able to make war with him?

In this study we have also seen that the armies of Russia and her allies will be defeated dramatically and supernaturally by God Himself when they invade Palestine. But before all of these things take place, God is going to call out His own from this world. We who are Christians, by virtue of the indwelling Holy Spirit, are a salt in the earth, slowing down the process of corruption. In fact, the full development of evil cannot be manifested until the Holy Spirit in the Church is taken out of the way. II Thessalonians 2:6, 7 declares,

> And now ye know what restraineth that he [Antichrist] might be revealed in his time.

For the mystery of iniquity doth already work; only he who now hindereth will continue to hinder until he [the Holy Spirit] be taken out of the way.

We are not looking for the Antichrist. We are not awaiting the fulfillment of Ezekiel 38 and 39. We are, however, expecting the appearance of our Savior.

And now, little children, abide in him, that, when he shall appear, we may have confidence and not be ashamed before him at his coming (I John 2:28).

Chapter Ten

THE TIME OF RUSSIA'S OVERTHROW

Russia and a number of allied nations will suffer an overwhelming and dramatic defeat at the hand of God when they invade the land of Palestine. We have seen that this is clearly predicted in Ezekiel 38 and 39, and there is no doubt that this prophetic picture has not yet been fulfilled. No coalition of nations from the extreme north of Palestine has ever become the object of God's penal wrath, and suffered a supernatural destruction of its armies as is described in Ezekiel 38:18-23. Furthermore, Ezekiel specifically states that it will take place in "the latter years" (Ezekiel 38:8), and in "the latter days" (Ezekiel 38:16). We are completely justified, therefore, in expecting a future fulfillment of this prophecy.

FIRST THE RAPTURE

We should not look for it to be realized while the Church is still on earth. The "latter days" and "latter years" of Israel's history will not begin until the Church has been removed from the earthly scene. Not until then will God once again deal with the Jews as a nation in a direct and supernatural manner. Especially serious is the error some make when they insist that this prophecy *must* be fulfilled *before* the rapture. If one believes this he will cease looking for the any-moment return of Jesus Christ. He will look instead for the supernatural destruction of the armies of Russia and her allies when they attempt an invasion of Palestine.

SIXTY-NINE WEEKS FULFILLED

We believe when one has a clear picture of God's prophetic program he can determine the exact place of this earth-shattering event in God's timetable. Therefore, let us briefly review the general outline of future events as they are depicted in Daniel 9. An understanding of Daniel 9: 20-27 is all-important if one is going to properly interpret the prophetic Scriptures. God told Daniel, "Seventy weeks are determined upon *thy people* [the Jews] and upon *thy holy city* [Jerusalem]," before the glorious Messianic Kingdom is to be established.

> Know, therefore, and understand, that from the going forth of the commandment to restore and to build Jerusalem unto the Messiah, the Prince, shall be seven weeks, and threescore and two weeks; the street shall be built again, and the wall, even in troublous times.
>
> And after threescore and two weeks shall Messiah be cut off, but not for himself; and the people of the prince that shall come shall destroy the city and the sanctuary, and the end of it shall be with a flood, and unto the end of the war desolations are determined.
>
> And he shall confirm the covenant with many for one week; and in the midst of the week he shall cause the sacrifice and the oblation to cease, and for the overspreading of abominations he shall make it desolate, even until the consummation, and that determined shall be poured upon the desolate (Daniel 9:25-27).

These "weeks" are seven-year periods, and history has demonstrated the accuracy of Daniel's predictions. "Messiah the Prince" (verse 25) presented Himself to the Jews as their Messiah exactly 483 years after the decree of

Artaxerxes, a precise fulfillment of the sixty-nine weeks. The Messiah [Jesus Christ] was "cut off" [crucified], and a few years later the city of Jerusalem and the temple were destroyed by the Romans. Thus the prophecies of verses 25 and 26 were fulfilled with amazing accuracy.

SEVENTIETH WEEK IS FUTURE

The last seven-year period of this prophecy has not yet been realized. Verse 27 tells us that a prominent figure will make an agreement or treaty with "the many" [Jews] for "one week" or seven years. He will not keep his covenant, however, for we are told that in the middle of this seven-year period he will suddenly turn against the Jews. The man who makes this agreement and then breaks it is clearly identified in the context. He is the second "prince" of Daniel 9:26. The first one is "Messiah, the Prince," and the second one is the "prince that shall come." His people, the Romans, destroyed the temple and the city of Jerusalem in A.D. 70. This "prince that shall come" is the future head of the revived Roman Empire, the western Ten-Nation Confederacy predicted in Daniel 2 and 7. He is the personage portrayed as the first "beast" in Revelation 13:1-10.

A HYPOCRITICAL "FRIEND"

This political genius will pose as a friend of the Jews for three and one-half years. He will apparently settle the Arab-Israeli controversy by granting Israel undisputed possession of Palestine, and the Jews in the land will be guaranteed protection from all foes. Thus the people of Israel will live in their land with a feeling of complete security.

These conditions will suddenly change, however, when the leader turns against the Jews, abolishes their worship, and inaugurates a period of intense persecution. Therefore, the last three and one-half years of the seventieth week will not find Israel dwelling securely. This is significant because Ezekiel 38:11 specifically declares that the northern coalition will come down upon Palestine when Israel is living in peace and safety.

> And thou shalt say, I will go up to the land of unwalled villages; I will go to those who are at rest, who dwell safely, all of them dwelling without walls, and having neither bars nor gates (Ezekiel 38:11).

MIDDLE OF THE SEVENTIETH WEEK

When we consider the fact that Israel today is in constant jeopardy because of fear that one of its neighboring nations will attack it, we certainly realize the situation is not right for the fulfillment of this prophecy. It is extremely unlikely that this condition will change until the head of the Western Confederacy of Nations predicted by Daniel as the "prince that shall come" assures Israel of his protection, and makes it known to the Arab neighbors. Isaiah spoke of this coming treaty between Israel and Antichrist, and called it "your agreement with sheol" (Isaiah 28:18). Therefore, inasmuch as this attack will come from the north when "they [Israel] shall dwell safely, all of them . . . dwelling without walls, and having neither bars nor gates . . ." (Ezekiel 38:8, 11), it must occur sometime *after* the Beast [Antichrist] makes this covenant with Israel and *before* he turns against them. This places it during the first half of the tribulation period, Daniel's seventieth week.

ANTICHRIST'S SUDDEN CHANGE EXPLAINED

There are some other considerations which lead us to believe that the defeat of Gog and Magog will occur near the middle of the tribulation period rather than in its early months.

In the first place, the sudden collapse of Russia as a military power explains the abrupt change in the attitude of the Beast to Israel. He will not be completely comfortable about the Middle East as long as Russia exists as a great hostile power. He will feel that he needs the friendship of the Jews. Therefore, he will pledge himself to defend Israel against the Arab nations. Apparently Russia and her allies will expect to fight a major war in the Middle East when they come down. They will be anticipating a clash not only with Israel, but also with the United Western powers. When God supernaturally destroys these invading forces before they join in battle with the armies of the Middle East, the way will be clear for Antichrist to assert himself as the absolute world ruler, and even to demand that mankind worship him. We know from Daniel 9 that this will occur in the middle of the seven-year period. This certainly indicates that Russia will be defeated very shortly before the mid-point of Daniel's seventieth week.

Antichrist will apparently produce an image of himself, place it in the temple of the Jews in Jerusalem, and demand that men worship him through this image or die. Speaking of the False Prophet, the religious leader who works with the Beast, Revelation 13:15 declares,

> And he hath power to give life unto the image of the beast, that the image of the beast should both speak, and cause that as many as would not worship the image of the beast should be killed.

Jesus referred to this same incident in His Olivet discourse when He said,

> When ye, therefore, shall see the abomination of desolation,

spoken of by Daniel the prophet, stand in the holy place (whosoever readeth, let him understand),

Then let them who are in Judaea flee into the mountains;

Let him who is on the housetop not come down to take anything out of his house;

Neither let him who is in the field return back to take his clothes (Matthew 24:15-18).

Russia's crushing defeat will trigger this sudden display of "power madness" on the part of the Beast. We know that from this point on he will continue as ruler for 42 months, according to Revelation 13:5 where we read, ". . . and power was given unto him to continue forty and two months." This places the fulfillment of the Gog and Magog prophecy very near the middle of the tribulation period.

A DRAMATIC SPIRITUAL RENEWAL

Another consideration that points to the middle of the "seventieth week" as the time for the fulfillment of this prophecy is found in the fact that many Jews and Gentiles will turn to God during the last half of the tribulation period. Ezekiel 39 tells us that as a consequence of the defeat of the northern powers,

. . . they shall know that I am the Lord.

So will I make my holy name known in the midst of my people, Israel, and I will not let them pollute my holy name any more; and the nations shall know that I am the Lord, the Holy One in Israel (Ezekiel 39:6, 7).

CRUEL PERSECUTION

Because of this recognition of God, Satan's ire will be aroused. This explains his bitter persecution of those who will not worship the image. Thousands of people will turn to the Lord and be willing to die for their faith. These martyred believers make up the great unnumbered multitude John pictures in Revelation 7:9-17, and who are specifically identified in verse 14,

> . . . These are they who came out of the great tribulation, and have washed their robes, and made them white in the blood of the Lamb.

A SERIOUS WARNING

The Apostle Paul also instructed us concerning the coming man of sin, and issues a solemn warning to those who have deliberately rejected Jesus Christ.

> And then shall that wicked one be revealed, whom the Lord shall consume with the spirit of his mouth, and shall destroy with the brightness of his coming,
> Even him whose coming is after the working of Satan with all power and signs and lying wonders,
> And with all deceivableness of unrighteousness in them that perish, because they received not the love of the truth, that they might be saved.
> And for this cause God shall send them strong delusion, that they should believe the lie,
> That they all might be judged who believed not the truth, but had pleasure in unrighteousness (II Thessalonians 2:8-12).

These verses indicate that, although among the nations many will turn to God, the majority of mankind will be deceived by the lies of Antichrist. Those who have been faced with the claims of Jesus Christ and have rejected Him will be among those deluded by the devil and his co-workers.

CONFIRMING SUMMATION

Thus we find that this defeat of Russia and her satellites near the middle of the seventieth week of Daniel perfectly dovetails into the prophetic picture as we find it revealed in the Scriptures. It meets the condition that Israel is dwelling in peace and safety when the invasion is launched. It explains the sudden change in Antichrist's policy, and shows us how with Russia out of the way he achieves his brief tenure as the unchallenged world leader. It also sheds light upon the conversion of multitudes of Gentiles, and the turning of Israel as a nation back to God.

It is obvious that this event cannot be the same as the Battle of Armageddon described in Zechariah 14 and Revelation 19:11-21, which comes at the end of the tribulation period, when Israel will be experiencing the bitterest time of its history. In contrast, Ezekiel 38:11 clearly declares that the invasion from the uttermost north takes place when Israel dwells in a feeling of security.

Some Bible students teach that this battle could occur early in the millennium, in the period of a few weeks while the Lord is organizing the Messianic Kingdom. It is true, of course, that a brief period of time will be involved before all weapons of warfare are destroyed and converted to implements for useful purposes. Daniel 12:11-13 indicates that there will be a period of 75 days after the destruction of the beast before the full blessings of the millennial age will be enjoyed. A few devout men believe that while the Lord is organizing affairs, and before the wicked have been judged, these powers from the extreme north will make a desperate attempt to destroy Israel and defeat the Lord Jesus. They point out that Israel will then fulfill the conditions of Ezekiel 38:11 because it will be dwelling in peace and safety.

However, two important considerations militate against this position. In the first place, Ezekiel 39:12 tells us that as an aftermath of the battle against Gog and Magog, the land will be defiled for seven months because of the dead bodies of slain men. This is not in keeping with the cleansing of the earth which will be accomplished by the return of Messiah. Secondly, Ezekiel 39:23-29 indicates that the final regathering and conversion of Israel *follows* the battle of Gog and Magog. In fact, verses 25 and 26 indicate that *both* Israel's *great suffering* and her *final blessing* will occur *after* this divine judgment upon the northern powers.

> Therefore, thus saith the Lord God: Now will I bring again the captivity of Jacob, and have mercy upon the whole house of Israel, and will be jealous for my holy name,
>
> *AFTER* they have borne their shame, and all their trespasses by which they have trespassed against me . . . (Ezekiel 39:25, 26).

Therefore, we conclude that Russia and her allies will be utterly defeated by the hand of God in the middle of the seventieth week of Daniel.

All about us we see evidence that the world is shaping up for the fulfillment of these final events in God's prophetic program. Yet we are not looking for the battle of Gog and Magog. We who know the Lord Jesus Christ, like the Thessalonian Christians,

> . . . wait for his Son from heaven, whom he raised from the dead, even Jesus, who delivered us from the wrath to come (I Thessalonians 1:10).

Chapter Eleven

THE MANNER OF RUSSIA'S OVERTHROW

In this series of chapters we have shown that the prophetic Scriptures tell us of two great end-time battles which will occur before the Kingdom of God is ushered in upon the earth. The first one is depicted by the Prophet Ezekiel, and can be found in the 38th and 39th chapters of his book. We have examined these chapters, and have found good reason to conclude that they describe the crushing military defeat of Russia and her allies by God's supernatural power, and that this will take place about three and one-half years after the Church is raptured, in the middle of the seventieth week of Daniel 9. The second divinely predicted battle of the end-time is described in many passages of Scripture, and is sometimes called the Battle of Armageddon. References to it may be found in Daniel 11:36-45; Zechariah 14:1-15; Revelation 16:13-16, and 19:11-16. This battle will involve a great gathering of armies from every part of the world as they meet in the valley of Megiddo in northern Israel for an attack upon Jerusalem. Megiddo today is about 14 miles wide and 20 miles long, and is a beautiful plain which would be very suitable for such a concentration of troops. They will be under the leadership of the head of the Western Confederacy of Nations. The Battle of Armageddon will occur about three and one-half years after the destruction of Russia, when the Lord will bring upon these armies the same supernatural devastation with which He visited the attackers from the uttermost north. This time Jesus Christ Himself will come down to earth, take the Throne of David, hold the judgment of the nations, and set up the millennial kingdom.

LITERAL INTERPRETATION NECESSARY

In this study we would like to center our attention again upon the first battle, and, considering some of the details found in Ezekiel 38 and 39, explain a few of the problems Bible students have faced in their consideration of these chapters.

Some have insisted it is absolutely impossible to interpret Ezekiel's words in a literal manner. They tell us these chapters are a clear indication that we should resort to a symbolical explanation of many Old Testament prophecies. We definitely believe, however, it is necessary to interpret prophecy literally, and it is not a mark of ignorance to expect these two chapters to be thus fulfilled.

DETAILS FULLY CLARIFIED AT FULFILLMENT

It is well to remember that prophecies can be real and meaningful, even though one may not understand every fine point, or be able to explain how each part will be fulfilled. We see this illustrated in the Old Testament passages concerning the first coming of Jesus Christ to the earth. They predicted Christ would be born in Bethlehem (Micah 5:2), of a virgin (Isaiah 7:14), at approximately the close of the sixty-nine sevens of years (Daniel 9:25). They prophesied that infants in Bethlehem would be massacred at this time (Jeremiah 31:15), and that He would somehow return to the land of Israel from Egypt (Hosea 11:1). They foretold His ministry in Galilee (Isaiah 9:1, 2), His rejection (Isaiah 53:3), His triumphal entry into Jerusalem riding upon a colt (Zechariah 9:9), His betrayal for 30 pieces of silver (Zechariah 11:12), and the return of this money for the purchase of a potter's field (Zechariah 11:13). Psalm 22 declared that he would cry out, "My God, My God, why hast thou forsaken me," that His hands and feet would be pierced, He would be mocked and reviled, and that lots would be cast for the possession of His outer garment. Isaiah 53 predicted He would suffer vicariously, would be silent when falsely accused, and that He would die with transgressors and yet be buried honorably in the grave of a rich man.

These, and many other details of our Lord's life, death and resurrection were prophesied in the Old Testament, and now, looking back upon them, we see how strikingly they were fulfilled. Yet, no Old Testament student could have fitted all these details together in advance to predict the exact manner and time they would be realized.

Thus it is with the prophecies we read concerning the end-time. The general picture is clear, even though a number of the fine points concerning their fulfillment may be hidden from us. Therefore, do not make the mistake of ignoring or disbelieving the prophetic Scriptures just because some details *seem* contradictory or impossible. God knows how He will work out all these particulars, and someday these prophecies will be as clear to us as those relating to the first advent of Jesus.

OBSOLETE EQUIPMENT

Questions have been raised about the fact that Ezekiel pictures the armies from the north as coming against Palestine riding upon horses and using antiquated weapons: shields, swords, spears, bows and arrows.

> . . . and I will bring thee forth, and all thine army, horses, and horsemen, all of them clothed with all sorts of armor, even a great company with bucklers and shields, all of them handling swords:
>
> Persia, Cush, and Put with them; all of them with shield and helmet (Ezekiel 38:4, 5).

Moreover, the vehicles and weapons are described as made largely of wood. Ezekiel tells us they will serve as firewood for a period of seven years, after the armies are destroyed by God.

> And they that dwell in the cities of Israel shall go forth, and shall set on fire and burn the weapons, both the shields and the bucklers, the bows and the arrows, and the hand-spikes, and the spears, and they shall burn them with fire seven years,
>
> So that they shall take no wood out of the field, neither cut down any out of the forests; for they shall burn the weapons with fire; and they shall spoil those that spoiled them, and rob those that robbed them, saith the Lord God (Ezekiel 39:9, 10).

In the light of our modern weapons of war, many have been puzzled as to how the description of this future battle, with its horses, bows and arrows, swords and shields, and wooden vehicles, must be understood. Does this mean it will be fought with such "antiquated" and "obsolete" weaponry? Let me say, first of all, we certainly should not give a symbolical interpretation to these predictions. Prophecy must be taken literally. A study of those prophecies which have already been fulfilled reveals this very clearly.

LANGUAGE OF HIS DAY

Some insist that God led Ezekiel to describe the armies in this coming battle in language familiar to himself and his contemporaries. He pictured well-equipped armies as they appeared in his day. The counterpart today would be troops featuring all kinds of mechanized vehicles and offensive weapons. The firewood used in that time would correspond to fuel which men employ today to run their motorized vehicles. In the recent war between Israel and its neighbors, the Israelis were able to capture great amounts of gasoline and oil left intact because of the speed with which they defeated the enemies. One can visualize vast quantities of fuel thus available to the inhabitants of Palestine when the invading forces are supernaturally and suddenly destroyed. Thus, the fulfillment of the prophecy would be literal, even though Ezekiel presented the picture in terms understandable to people who know nothing of modern-day weapons or vehicles.

Two Feasible Explanations

Another possibility is that these armies will actually come down upon Palestine riding horses and using primitive weapons. The nations may sign a disarmament treaty, and, with mutual inspection, no nation could produce tanks and guns without detection. However, it would be possible to quickly gather many horses in a land like Russia, and the rapid production of wooden weapons and equipment would be no problem. Armies thus equipped would certainly be able to overcome people who had no weapons of warfare at all. Some have also suggested, because we today have missiles that effectively seek, pursue, and destroy aircraft, it is possible the day will come when all mechanized equipment will be highly vulnerable. These missiles may become so effective that it will be futile to use motorized vehicles in warfare. This might cause these nations to turn back to the use of horses and wooden equipment. The fact is we cannot state dogmatically just how these details of Ezekiel's prophecy will be fulfilled, but we certainly need have no difficulty believing that God will be true to His Word.

SEVEN-MONTH BURIAL PROGRAM

Another problem that confronts some interpreters of Ezekiel 38 and 39 is the fact that after this great battle in which Russia will be defeated, the Israelites are pictured as burying the dead for a period of seven months. Here's the record in verses 12 through 16 of the 39th chapter,

> And seven months shall the house of Israel be burying them, that they may cleanse the land.
> Yea, all the people of the land shall bury them; and it shall be to their renown on the day that I shall be glorified, saith the Lord God.
> And they shall set apart men for the continual task of passing through the land to bury, with the help of the travelers, those that remain upon the face of the land, to cleanse it; after the end of seven months shall they make their search.
> And the travelers that pass through the land, when any seeth a man's bone, then shall he set up a sign by it, till the buriers have buried it in the Valley of Hamon-gog.
> And also the name of the city shall be Hamonah. Thus shall they cleanse the land (Ezekiel 39:12-16).

According to this prophecy, the people of Israel, joined by others, will be occupied in burying dead soldiers for seven months. After this time, most of the task will be completed, but some men will continue to be employed for the purpose of burying the human remains still present. Travelers through the land will assist by marking any spot where they discover a human bone or fragment.

THE PROBLEM AND A LIKELY SOLUTION

Because of the length of time involved in burying the dead, there are some expositors who claim that we cannot literally interpret these words. They point out that one million people, each one burying two corpses a day, would in the 180 working days of seven months, dispose of 360 million men. However, we must not jump to unnecessary conclusions simply because the Bible does not fill in all the details of this picture. First of all, remember, the earth during those days will be passing through the most turbulent time in all of its history. If we are correct in our conclusion that this defeat of Russia occurs about midway through the tribulation period, then it will be followed almost immediately by the world ruler's breaking of his treaty, the erection of his image for worship, and the bitter persecution of those who refuse to bow to it.

Moreover, the devastating and frightening judgments from Heaven depicted in the book of Revelation will fall upon the earth. No doubt these conditions will cause many interruptions which will delay this unpleasant task of burying the dead soldiers from the north, causing the project to span seven months of time. Therefore, though both Jews ["the house of Israel," verse 12] and Gentiles of various nationalities ["all the people of the land," verse 13] are involved in the work, it is not at all difficult to see how seven months will elapse before the disposal of these dead corpses is completed. We who believe God's Word, even though we might not explain just how this prophecy will be fulfilled, have every confidence in the veracity of God and in His ability to bring about the realization of Ezekiel's prophecy.

God's Answer to Despairing Men

We are living in an age of pessimism and despair. The lawlessness and reckless pursuit of earthly pleasures all about us are symptoms of the spiritual sickness of mankind;

and most thinking people, even those who are not Christians, are painfully aware of this fact. Unsaved people who seriously contemplate the future see no hope for the individual, nor for the human race. Many of them believe we are approaching the midnight hour, and quietly predict that man will one day soon destroy himself through drugs or nuclear war. The people who talk in glowing terms about a warless and classless world are theorists who are not facing reality. Without God, the God who speaks in the Bible, man is doomed both individually and collectively. In sharp contrast, we who believe the Bible are not hopeless nor living in the dark. We know that the same God who for centuries told men He would send the Savior to pay the price for sin and conquer death, and then fulfilled His promise, will also carry out every promise He has made to us. He has granted to every believer in Jesus Christ the forgiveness of sins, a new life, and the possibility of victory over sin. In the Bible He tells us that Jesus Christ is coming again to take us unto Himself. He has also given to us a picture of the means He will use to lead the people of Israel to the acceptance of their Messiah. He has revealed to us the manner and time that the powerful communistic nations will be destroyed. He has described how the great Western Roman Empire will be re-established, and how the massed armies from this entire federation of nations will be destroyed by the personal intervention of Jesus Christ when He comes to the earth to establish the millennial kingdom.

God's Supernatural Power Displayed

Man is having his little day. In patience, God permits puny and insignificant humans to ridicule and blaspheme His Name. But remember this, the destiny of every person and every nation is in His omnipotent hands. One day, perhaps very soon, man's little time will end. The "Day of the Lord" will arrive. God will step in and manifest His great power openly before all the world. The Church will be caught up. Following this, the powers of evil will seem to have absolute freedom here upon earth, but God will be working in a marvelous manner. During this seven-year tribulation period after the Church has been raptured, multitudes will turn to Jesus Christ. Yes, God will permit Antichrist to achieve great power, but all along He will be displaying the fact that He is in absolute control. He will supernaturally destroy the armies of Russia and her allies about midway through the tribulation period. He will then pour out His wrath upon this wicked Christ-rejecting world. Then, when the armies from all the nations combine to make their final onslaught upon those who are true to God, Jesus Christ will come again and bring justice, order, prosperity, and peace to this troubled world. Jesus Christ will reign over all the earth. He will be acknowledged as Lord of Lord and King of Kings. We who know Him will be safe in Glory, and we shall share in His rule. What a glorious prospect is ours!

> Jesus shall reign where'er the sun
> Does his successive journeys run;
> His kingdom spread from shore to shore,
> Till moons shall wax and wane no more.

DO YOU KNOW HIM?

If you do not know Him, however, you have no such future to anticipate. In order to share in the blessedness of the Lord's coming, it is imperative that you receive Him as your Savior. Jesus died on the cross to pay the price for your sins, and God will freely forgive you if you place your trust in Him.

> For by grace are ye saved through faith; and that not of yourselves, it is the gift of God:
> Not of works, lest any man should boast (Ephesians 2:8, 9).

Have you ever been born again? If not, you can know, right now, the reality of this new life in Christ Jesus. Why not bow your head and utter this simple prayer of faith? Say, "Lord Jesus, I know that I am a sinner and could never save myself. I believe You died for me and shed Your blood for my sin, and that You rose again from the dead. And now I am receiving You as my Savior, my Lord, my only hope of salvation. Lord, be merciful to me a sinner, and save me according to the promise of Your Word. Amen."

If you prayed this and really meant it, you are saved. The Bible says,

> *For whosoever shall call upon the name of the Lord shall be saved* (Romans 10:13).